THE RISE AND FALL OF CIVILISATION

Books by Shepard B. Clough

THE RISE AND FALL OF CIVILISATION
MAKING FASCISTS: *with Herbert W. Schneider*
HISTORY OF THE FLEMISH MOVEMENT IN BELGIUM
FRANCE, 1789-1939. A STUDY IN NATIONAL ECONOMICS
AN ECONOMIC HISTORY OF EUROPE: *with Charles W. Cole*
A CENTURY OF AMERICAN LIFE INSURANCE

THE RISE AND FALL OF CIVILISATION

An Inquiry into the Relationship between Economic Development and Civilisation

SHEPARD B. CLOUGH

SKEFFINGTON
Stratford Place
London

Skeffington and Son Limited
Founded in 1858
London   New York   Toronto
Melbourne   Sydney   Cape Town

First published in Great Britain 1953

Printed in Great Britain by
Cheltenham Press Ltd.
Cheltenham and London.

To
TONY and PETE

PREFACE

Publisher 5.00

3/87/63

TO explain the rise and fall of civilisation in several cultures, as I have attempted to do in the pages of this book, is a formidable task, and in retrospect I wonder that I ever had the courage to undertake it. I believed, however, that I could clarify what in Western Europe and America is meant by civilisation, that I could throw light upon the major factors in the rises and falls of civilisation, and that I might discover some pattern in these fluctuations. I felt that the Western world was anxiously groping for a fuller comprehension of these issues but that this understanding could not be obtained, at least not by the general public, from existing literature. Indeed some of this literature, particularly the work of Arnold J. Toynbee, seemed to me to obscure human experience rather than to make it clear.

In my study I have not attempted to present a great mass of evidence but have rather introduced evidence in an abbreviated form in the hope that the reader may be able to grasp its significance relative to the subject being investigated. Such condensation is extremely difficult to accomplish without doing injustice to the data or without arousing the suspicions of specialists. I have striven always to avoid distortion and have had the assistance of experts, notably that of McGregor Gray, for those parts of the study for which I could claim no special competence.

Any work of the kind presented here is based upon the total intellectual experience of the author. Accordingly, he owes a debt to those teachers whom he has known personally and to those whom he has known exclusively through their writings. Among the former I wish to pay homage especially to Carlton J. H. Hayes, William L. Westermann, Henri Sée, and Charles A. Beard. Among the latter I acknowledge my indebtedness to those who have endeavoured by empirical means and by verification to understand human behaviour.

For the research which has gone into this book I have made use of the remarkable resources of the Nicholas Murray Butler Library of Columbia University and of the excellent collections in the Dartmouth College Library, which have been available to me for more summers than I wish to count. To the staff of both of these institutions I express my sincere thanks.

SHEPARD B. CLOUGH

CONTENTS

CONTENTS

MAPS

I

A FOREWORD

FEW questions of our times have aroused more curiosity than the rise and fall of what are commonly called civilisations, for modern man is witnessing great changes in the relative economic, political, artistic, and intellectual positions of various peoples of the earth. He is seeing Western Europe lose its place of world dominance which was so clearly established at the time of European expansion overseas in the sixteenth century. He is observing the once-great Eastern cultures bowed down by war, poverty, and over-population. And he is witnessing an enormous growth of power and intellectual activity in Russia and in the United States. Being of an inquiring mind, modern man seeks an explanation of what is going on around him—some orderly description and analysis of what is taking place. He wants a comprehensible and usable concept of what civilisation is, a yardstick for measuring its rises and falls, and information regarding those factors that contribute to its fluctuations.

The problem stated

Existing literature provides little light on these subjects, at least not in concise form. Many authors who have addressed themselves to the question of civilisation have shied away from even an attempt to define civilisation and hence have failed to make clear what forces contribute to upward or downward trends of achievement. This is largely true of Arnold J. Toynbee, whose

The Study of History (1934 *ff.*) has received extensive attention since World War II. He employs such clichés as "challenge and response" and "withdrawal and return" to explain what leads to higher or lower stages of civilisation, but he fails to indicate what "challenges" in what circumstances have elicited what "responses," or what effect a "withdrawal" of a culture has in determining a "return."

Similarly Oswald Spengler, whose *The Decline of the West* (1926–1928) had a remarkable vogue after World War I, is vague concerning a concept of civilisation, and he confuses the issue of civilising forces by drawing an analogy between the life cycle of a living organism and that of a culture. Both presumably are born, have a youth, mature, grow old, and die, which, if true, would provide no casual explanation of the phenomenon before us. In fact, societies are not organisms and do not behave like them.

Other authors attribute change in degrees of civilisation primarily to some single factor, like geography, as does Ellsworth Huntington in his *Man and Civilisation* (1945), and thereby over-simplify what is extremely complex. Still others, who avoid many of these pitfalls, like Alfred L. Kroeber in his *Configurations of Culture* (1944), make no serious attempt to analyse the relation-ships between the economic well-being of a people and gradations of civilisation.

Because of these lacunae, and particularly the last, an his-torical inquiry into the rise and fall of civilisation primarily in its economic aspects seems a legitimate enterprise for an economic historian. But before embarking upon the historical phase of this study, it is essential, as in all scientific work, to state as clearly and as precisely as possible the object of the investigation. Thus at the very outset the author must endeavour to explain what is generally meant by the term civilisation. Although the word is relatively new, being derived from the concept of people living together according to accepted customs, that is, of acting civilly, it has acquired within the last 150 years a different and broader connotation. It refers to achievements in such aesthetic and intellectual pursuits as architecture, painting, literature, sculpture, music, philosophy, and science and to the success that a people has in establishing control over its human and physical environment. The greater the extent to which a people produces aesthetic and intellectual works of high merit and provides physical and social security for its members, the more civilised that people is; and conversely the less a people realizes either qualitatively or quantitatively any of these tenets of civilisation, the less civilised it is.

Various aspects of this definition of civilisation require elucidation. First, the term "people" needs to be made more precise, for we are not concerned with any heterogeneous conglomeration of human beings, but with people living in society, that is, with humans who are involved in a complex of relationships which grow out of action to attain common ends, including that of perpetuating the society. More specifically attention will be focused on societies that comprise cultures or, stated differently, with societies that have a body of learnable and transmissible knowledge the fundamental parts of which are homogeneous enough and firmly enough held to effect similarly and sharply the behaviour of a large number of persons. Thus we shall speak of French, German, or American societies and of Western culture of which these societies are parts.

Second, this definition of civilisation is one that comes from Western culture and from certain other prominent cultures during periods of their most brilliant accomplishments. It involves a value judgment which is not shared by all cultures. In fact, members of some societies have diametrically opposed conceptions of civilisation, for they consider the highest form of human existence to be a condition in which man does no work and receives the necessities of life from a bountiful and unfailing nature.

Third, attention should be called to the fact that in the

definition of a culture such qualitative and relative words as "homogeneous" and "similar" appear. One may well ask what amount of homogeneity or what degree of similarity must exist among people to justify distinguishing them as a culture. In whatever answer is given to this question an element of arbitrariness must enter, for there are no precise measures or standards of differentiation. All can recognize a profound difference between the behaviour of New Yorkers and Eskimos, of English and Chinese, and of French and Russians, yet one can observe considerable overlappings in the behaviour of the last two peoples and a twilight zone between Western and Eastern European cultures.

Fourth, we must realize that in estimating the degree of civilisation in any culture at a given time there is a nice problem of weighing different kinds of achievement. For example, is the degree of civilisation in a culture higher where great aesthetic works are being produced but where individual security does not exist than where these conditions are completely reversed ? This is a difficult matter to resolve, but reasonable conclusions can be obtained by comparing the degree to which all the tenets of civilisation are met by a culture at various periods of time. Similarly, the measurement of the greatness of a work of art is extremely difficult, for who can determine the respective beauties of an Egyptian vase and a Grecian urn ? In this matter we shall adopt the arbitrary procedure of considering to be of a higher order those things that have been most generally and most consistently recognized by competent authorities to be great.

Last, we must recognize that neither cultures nor civilisations are static but on the contrary are ever changing. Thus Greek culture, although it displayed a continuity of certain ideologies over a long period of time, was not a fixed entity, nor was the degree of civilisation attained by Athens in the fifth and fourth centuries B.C. attained by all the Greek city-states at the same moment or maintained by Athens for an indefinite space of time.

Why such changes took place and what has accounted for shifts
in centres of civilisation are problems in which we are interested.
Our findings should throw light upon what is happening within
Western culture today, upon the recent rise of Russia, and upon
the predicament in which Eastern cultures find themselves.

Factors in achieving higher degrees of civilisation

Having stated the primary theme of this study and having
discussed the term civilisation and its components, we turn to a
consideration of some of the major conditions that have contributed to the achievement of higher levels of civilisation. Of all
of these conditions none seems to be more fundamental than the
possession of economic surplus, that is, of agricultural goods,
industrial products, and various services in excess of what is
immediately necessary for the maintenance of life. Obviously
only when the necessities of physical existence have been provided
can energies be devoted to creative enterprise of an aesthetic
and intellectual character or can physical security be assured.
This is true even in those periods when wealth has been highly
concentrated in the hands of a few who supported artists and
intellectuals in one way or another and provided at least a
modicum of security against want and violence as well as in
those times when relatively extensive economic well-being existed
throughout society.

The idea that relative economic well-being in society is one
of the most necessary conditions to a high stage of civilisation
leads to an exceedingly appealing hypothesis regarding the fluctuating character of civilisation within a culture—a hypothesis
which is much more impelling than Toynbee's "challenge and
response" or Spengler's analogy. This hypothesis, succinctly
stated, is that as a large proportion of human energies in a culture
is devoted to the achievement and enjoyment of great works of
art—that is, achieving a higher civilisation—the smaller the proportion of energies which will be available for creating economic

well-being—that is, in creating a necessary condition in the process of civilisation. This hypothesis, which admittedly points to only one of many factors that contribute to fluctuations in civilisation, would lead to two further hypotheses: (1) that the peak of civilisation in any culture would be expected at the time when economic decline begins and (2) that the prolongation of high states of civilisation can be achieved by a nice balance in the utilization of human energies between aesthetic and economic activity.

In any case, the evidence presented in the pages of this book supports the contention that economic surplus has contributed to advances in civilisation, although some of these contributions have been indirect. For example, one of the major concomitants of economic well-being has been trade, and trade has been essential in promoting exchanges of ideas among peoples and in providing creative stimuli through economic and cultural competition. Economic surplus presupposes considerable business activity, and great business enterprise implies the keeping of business records. In fact, it was in keeping records of business that the earliest known forms of writing were used, that the first condensed systems of numerical notation were conceived, and that the most ancient calendars were developed. Furthermore, business has employed artists to design its products, architects to plan buildings to house its operations, and intellectuals of various kinds to help it produce what people want.

Lastly, economic surplus has made urbanization possible, which is of great moment because the outstanding achievements of civilisation have been products of urban centres. In fact, the aesthetic creations of various cultures have been so highly concentrated in cities that the treasures of places like Athens, Rome, and Paris are regarded as epitomes of their respective cultures.

The role of cities in the process of civilisation is to be accounted for in part by the fact that in urban centres a larger number of persons than in rural areas has had time over and above that required for meeting the material needs of life to devote to devising ways to extend man's control over his environment and to engage in cultural activity. Recent studies of cultural influence confirm the historical observation of the dominant role of cities. In fact, they indicate that there is a distinct correlation between cultural influence on the one hand and size of city and commercial activity on the other, that the influence of the city wanes with effective distance,[1] and that the greater the economic dependence upon cities, the greater is the influence of urban centres.[2] Plans for the realization of the most generally recognized triumphs of science, engineering, sculpture, music, architecture, painting, and literature have been produced in cities or by persons who received the stimuli for their work in urban areas. Also the process of acculturation—the borrowing of knowledge, ideas, techniques, forms of organization, art styles, and ideals towards which society should strive—has taken place primarily in cities and has radiated from them.

Essential as economic surplus may have been in providing leisure for the civilising process, basic as trade has been for the diffusion of ideas, and important as has been the role of cities as centres of cultural achievement, the place of economic factors in the rise and fall of civilisation must not be exaggerated. In fact, of equal, if not of greater, importance are the controlling ideologies of a culture. These principles become established chiefly in periods of great and rapid change, as at the very beginning of a culture. At such times goals, intellectual standards, art forms, and technological attitudes become differentiated and specialized. If in this stage the culture embraces the idea that great works of art should be created, that knowledge of the universe should be acquired, and that man should extend his control over human and physical environment, then subsequently more of the energies of the culture will be devoted to the attainment of a higher degree of civilisation than would otherwise be the case.

What leads to the adoption of such an ideology is difficult to determine. It may be borrowed from some other culture, or it may be developed indigenously. In the latter case climatic and geographic elements may have an influence, for a too bounteous nature may be conducive to sloth, while a too hostile environment may permit of no leisure. Possibly a climate with wide seasonal fluctuations is of importance, for it requires that a surplus be stored during the productive months to tide one over the unproductive months of the year; and this practice provides leisure for other than the obtaining of sustenance. Furthermore natural resources have something to do with the case, because a relatively barren land would not permit the accumulation of surplus. At all events most of the great civilisations which we know have been mainly in temperate regions, and there has been a tendency for the highest civilisations to move towards more invigorating, colder, and stormier areas.

Another ideology that is important for the effective development of civilisation is a desire for a social and political organization that will permit individuals to realize their total potential as contributors to civilisation. What is implied here is that in a system where social taboos or political restrictions prevent large segments of a culture's population from engaging in types of activity that add most to civilisation, the culture cannot attain the highest degree of civilisation of which it is capable. Thus the caste system in India, restrictions on choice of occupation in medieval Europe, and the anti-Semitic laws of Nazi Germany curtailed the civilising process. Also implied in the foregoing statement is freedom from destructive strife, for obviously civilisation is retarded if man uses his energies for destroying what has been built rather than for building anew. In general, ravaging warfare has preceded a decline in civilisation, for cultures with a high degree of civilisation have aroused the envy of, and have become the object of attack by, less favoured cultures.

Lastly, among factors conducive to the achievement of higher forms of civilisation, mention should be made of a good state of health in the population, the propagation of those elements in society that have the ability to produce offspring with good physiological equipment for creative activity, a balance between production and population so that an increase in people does not absorb all the potential for economic surplus, and the placing of leadership in the hands of those who would advance civilisation rather than some other cause.

Of great importance also is the prevention of such a rigid structuring of the culture that the individual has no choice of action. Although there is evidence to indicate that some rigidities, let us say styles in art, tend to be fulfilled, that is, become so stereotyped that they are destroyed, others may last a long time and limit thought and aesthetic expression. Indeed the *range of opportunities for alternative decisions* is a useful concept in analysing civilising forces. Everything that contributes to the extension of that range, whether it be economic surplus, the use of leisure, the development of cities, or the absence of stultifying rigidities, is of the utmost significance in furthering the process of civilisation.

Factors of economic progress

Now that consideration has been given to what civilisation in various cultures is and to what factors have contributed to its development, especial attention is to be focused on economic progress. Indeed economic achievement in relation to degrees of civilisation will be a basic concern in the subsequent pages of this study. By economic progress is meant an increase in output of goods and services per capita in a society. Factors of economic progress may be grouped under the following headings: (1) natural resources, (2) technology and techniques of production, (3) labour, (4) capital, (5) business leadership and economic institutions, (6) demand for goods and techniques of distribution. An explanation for the location of economic activity in one area rather than in another is to be found primarily in terms of the extent to which these factors are present at a given place.

Inasmuch as frequent references to these elements of economic progress will be made in the following discussion of the rise and fall of civilisation, brief treatment of each of them here will save subsequent digressions from the main story. This treatment begins logically with natural resources. They are products of nature which can be utilized by man to satisfy material wants.

Accordingly a product of nature is not a natural resource until man has the knowledge, skill, means, and desire to utilize it for his own purposes.

Copper was not a natural resource until man learned to work it into useful articles about 3500 B.C. The same can be said of iron (*circa* 1300 B.C.), and of coal before the seventeenth or eighteenth century, when it first began to be used on a relatively large scale. Hence the value of the products of nature has varied widely as man has developed an ability to use one or the other of them.

This has even been true of agricultural land, perhaps the chief natural resource, as man learned to domesticate animals and plants, to drain and irrigate, and to transport bulky goods over long distances. Forests, which may have been barriers to settlement before sharp axes for felling trees were available, became important natural resources as more charcoal was needed for smelting. In fact, the abundance of timber in Western Europe gave that area an advantage over the relatively treeless areas of North Africa and Hither Asia and accounts in part for the shift in the centre of civilisation from the Mediterranean to the northward.[3] In more recent times power-producing natural resources, especially coal, have had a particularly strategic importance in economic progress, areas with the largest amount of coal available for use in industry having scored the greatest measure of industrialization.[4] In general, it may be said that the economic development of an area is conditioned by the amount and accessibility of its natural exploitable[5] resources per capita of the population.

The second condition of economic progress listed above is technology of production, that is, the body of abilities possessed by mankind to turn out goods and services. A technique, by comparison, is a particular way of accomplishing a stated task. In all cultures some of the existing technology has been inherited or borrowed from other cultures, and some has been developed or discovered indigenously. In this regard it should be noted that no major technical advance has ever been completely lost, even though some have remained dormant for long periods of time.

In the process of borrowing or acculturation the thing that is borrowed and put to use is determined primarily by the borrower's state of technology, by natural resources, by market demand, relative costs of production, available financing, and labour supply. In the spread of mechanized industry at the time of the industrial revolution in England in the eighteenth century, cotton textile machines were frequently the first to be adopted in other countries because the manner of operating them was similar to handicraft methods; raw material was frequently obtained by other areas as easily as by England; the demand for cotton textiles was great; and costs of the equipment were not high. At the same time new methods of iron production moved first to those inhabited areas in which natural resources were abundant and where some knowledge of iron-working already existed.

In invention and discovery the same factors come into play. Most of the great inventions and discoveries have been worked upon simultaneously and often independently by persons in separate but similar environments; they have resulted from the slow accretion of many details from many sources; and they have been applied first where "circumstances were favourable" for

their use.[6] Technology and techniques are basic to any understanding of economic progress, for they provide the most important means by which mankind can produce more goods and
services with less expenditure of human energy.

The third condition of economic progress is the capacity of
the individual worker. Capacity depends upon mastery of techniques, health, morale, and the division of labour, that is, the
specialization of workers in the production of some particular
part of an object rather than in the production of the whole
object. Indeed, cultures with the highest gross product per capita
have been those in which a large proportion of the labour force
has been engaged in industry, commerce, and transport, which
are branches of economic activity permitting a great division of
labour among workers and among geographical regions.[7] Still
another consideration here is the recompense obtained by workers
for their labour, for workers must be paid enough so that their
demands for goods will be effective in bringing forth greater
supplies.[8] Yet it is essential that there be savings from wages or
profits so that investment in additional economic enterprise will
continue to take place.[9]

The fourth condition of economic progress is capital. Capital
may be defined as valuables in the form of land, tools, machines,
buildings, materials, securities, money, or other transferables that
can be employed for the production of more goods and services.
The more abundant and the more mobile (quickly transferable)
capital is, the more readily it can be employed to take advantage
of opportunities for production. Consequently the development
of symbols that represent wealth, like the deed, mortgage, bond,
stock, and money, are of extreme importance in facilitating
transfer of ownership.

Of all these symbols of wealth the most important has undoubtedly been money. In fact, money has been classed as one
of the most fundamental finds in history, ranking close to the
discovery of fire, the domestication of grains and animals, writing,

and the use of machine-produced power. As a medium of exchange and as a store of wealth money has been more useful than all other forms in transferring wealth, in accumulating capital, and in permitting a division of labour. As our story progresses we shall have occasion to consider capital formation, growing reliance upon money in the exchange of goods, and the development of organs for the accumulation and investment of capital, like banks and stock exchanges.

The fifth condition of economic progress has to do with business leadership. In general the issue of leadership seems to boil down to this: men are born with biological equipment which may be extremely poor or exceptionally good; this biological equipment develops and acts primarily in response to stimuli from environment; and leaders are distinguished from other men in the degree to which stimuli effect creative responses. Thus in economic activity leaders are recognized by the extent to which they have been able to combine factors of production to turn out more goods and services.

What they have been able to accomplish is determined in part by the conditions of economic progress here under consideration, but their task has always been easier when cultural ideologies have been favourable to their aims. Thus business leaders have had an easier row to hoe when within society there has been a general conviction that it was well to increase the output of goods and services than when such production, or participation in such production, was scorned as socially and ethically degrading. Similarly economic progress has been enhanced by a generally accepted belief that economic energies should be exerted to produce capital goods (goods which could produce more goods) or consumer goods and services which improve physical well-being.

The sixth and last group of conditions of economic progress embraces the demand for goods and the technology of distribution. We have already touched on this subject in discussing labour and in that connection emphasized the need for sufficient remuneration to permit labour to be a high consumer. Clearly a large demand for goods is a stimulus to the production of more goods. This large demand may come in part from such a distribution of wealth that purchasing power is not concentrated in the hands of a few whose wants are surfeited with supply. It may come from popularizing the desirability of more goods and services like a radio in every room. And it may come, indeed it frequently has, from tapping markets in distant lands never before supplied with certain products. But a large market implies not only effective demand, that is, desire plus the ability to acquire goods, but also the means of effecting exchange and of transport. Money we have listed as particularly important in exchange, and we shall see later what wonders of distribution money made possible as compared to the system of barter. But in commerce we should not minimize the importance of credit, selling organizations like the store, and especially means of transportation. The use of the wheel as against packs and sledges, of hard-surfaced roads and rails as opposed to trails and dirt-roads, of the steam vessel compared to the oar-propelled boat, of the railway as against the ox-cart—these at once indicate the enormous advances that technological change has wrought in the exchange of goods and the division of labour, and thus in the history of economic development and of civilisation itself.

In what has preceded, particular stress has been placed upon factors for advances in civilisation and for progress in economic affairs—upon what is in general "environment." This raises the age-old question whether important developments in history have really been the result of "social forces," that is, environment, or whether they have been the result of "great men," that is, leaders. This question requires explanation. Obviously all human accomplishments have been realized by human effort; and the greater the individual accomplishment, the greater the man or men who were responsible for it. Yet the creations of great men have been limited by "conditions" of the time and place in which they lived. Thus one would not expect the invention of calculus to have been made by men of limited intelligence or by a thousand men at any one time and place, yet it is not surprising that two or three "great men" at about the same time and within the same civilisation invented calculus quite independently of each other. Environment and "great men" seem to be mutually interdependent, with "great men" working on environment to understand, control, or change it, and with a changing environment stimulating, challenging, and limiting the creative responses of these men.

Still another question arises from the material presented concerning factors for the development of civilisation or for economic progress; and that is whether or not a single factor can be isolated as the prime moving force. An affirmative answer to this question is especially tempting because it would enormously simplify analysis and control of social relations. Unfortunately, however, such a simplification would vitiate available evidence. The list of factors which I have made seems to be an irreducible minimum, although in specific cases one or another condition may be predominant. How this was will be seen as we proceed with the story.

FOOTNOTES TO CHAPTER I

1 Effective distance means actual distance augmented by impediments to transportation and communication, like mountains, swamps, or seas.

2 John Q. Stewart, "Empirical Mathematical Rules Concerning the Distribution and Equilibrium of Population," *The Geographical Review*, Vol. xxxvii, No. 3, 1947, pp. 461–485.

3 Ellen C. Semple, *Geography of the Mediterranean Region*, Henry Holt and Company, Inc., New York, 1931, Chap. XI. Also Graham Clark, "Forest Clearance and Prehistoric Farming," *The Economic History Review*, Vol. xvii, No. 1, 1947, pp. 45–52.

4 In the United States in 1937, 52 per cent. of energy used for heat and power was from coal, 32 per cent. from petroleum, 10 per cent. from natural gas, 4 per cent. from water, and the remainder from wood, wind, etc. It has been estimated that 97 per cent. of the energy used was provided by machines

and animals and 3 per cent. by humans. The United States used 1·6 times more energy per capita than the United Kingdom, 2·5 times more than Germany, 11 times more than Japan and 250 times more than China. *Energy Resources and National Policy. National Resources Committee*, Government Printing Office, Washington, 1939, p. 41.

5 The word "exploitable" is used to imply that the population has the knowledge and skill necessary for utilizing the resources.

6 S. C. Gilfillan, *The Sociology of Invention*, Follett Publishing Co., Chicago, 1935, and *Technological Trends and National Policy. National Resources Committee*, Government Printing Office, Washington, 1937.

7 Colin Clark, *Conditions of Economic Progress*, Macmillan & Co. Ltd., London, 1940, pp. 29 and 179.

8 *Industrialization and Foreign Trade*, League of Nations, New York, 1945, p. 116.

9 John Maurice Clark, "The Relation of Wages to Progress," *The Conditions of Industrial Progress*, Industrial Research Department, University of Pennsylvania, Philadelphia, 1947.

For Further Reading

Brooks Adams, *The Law of Civilisation and Decay* (1895)
Charles A. Beard, *The Making of American Civilisation* (1942)
A. M. Carr-Saunders, *World Population* (1936)
Colin Clark, *The Conditions of Economic Progress* (1951)
S. C. Gilfillan, *The Sociology of Invention* (1935)
Ellsworth Huntington, *Man and Civilisation* (1945)
Alfred L. Kroeber, *Configurations of Culture* (1944)
Ralph Linton, *The Science of Man in the Changing World* (1945)
R. M. MacIver, *Society: Its Structure and Changes* (1931)
―――― *The Web of Government* (1947)
R. D. McKenzie, *The Metropolitan Community* (1933)
Flinders Petrie, *The Revolutions of Civilisation* (1941)
Pitrim A. Sorokin, *Social Philosophies in an Age of Crisis* (1950)
Oswald Spengler, *The Decline of the West* (1926–1928), 2 Vols.
Arnold J. Toynbee, *The Study of History* (1934–1939), 6 Vols.
   One-volume abridgment by D. C. Somervell (1947).

II

THE EARLIEST CULTURES

THE planet on which we live, it is thought, was created by
the congealing of gases trillions of years ago. Over an estimated
billion and a half years ago the earth mass cooled and contracted,
developing folds and continents. Sometime, perhaps 1,000,000 or
500,000 years ago, man appeared on this globe. In the neighbourhood of 3000 B.C. man had developed civilisation to a point at
which written records were made—records that have come down
to us of the present day. Thus the last 5,000 years, or less than
one per cent. of man's existence, is to be the primary concern
of this study.

Limitations of our study in time and space

Even in this small fraction of man's total time on earth,
human beings have created such a vast and complex body of
records about themselves that one man cannot possibly cope with
it. Consequently from among the thousands of cultures about
which information is available, we shall select for study those
that have contributed most directly and in the largest measure
to the development of Western culture. Thus attention will be
focused primarily upon the cultures of Sumer, Egypt, Babylon,
the Aegean, Greece, Rome, and Western Europe.[1] Furthermore,
we shall not treat all phases of these cultures but shall stick to
a central theme—to see how various factors of economic progress

developed, to judge whether or not certain forces resulted in an increase in the production of goods and services per capita, and to suggest the relationship between economic progress and the achievement of higher levels of civilisation. In the present chapter we shall consider certain basic accomplishments which started man on the long road to greater control over his environment and to the creation of objects for intellectual and aesthetic enjoyment. More specifically we shall be concerned with technological changes that permitted the creation of economic surplus, with the division of labour and the growth of trade, with the establishment of cities, and with the development of writing and numerical notations.

Palaeolithic civilisation and the Neolithic agricultural revolution

When the earliest form of man appeared on this planet, he probably lived much like a wild animal. Although we lack information concerning his earliest economy, archaeological evidence seems to indicate that 140,000 years ago, as the last glacial period was approaching, man was a food gatherer rather than a food producer. He hunted game, sought fruit and nuts, and collected the seeds of plants for grain. He relied similarly on such products of nature as caves for shelter and on animal skins for clothing.

In the course of time man added to the technology by which he sustained life. He commenced to make use of fire and probably developed ways of producing it. He chipped pieces of stone from rocks in order to get weapons and tools with which to perform his elementary tasks more effectively and more expeditiously. Stone implements, which gave this earliest form of civilisation its name of Palaeolithic or Old Stone Age, were gradually improved in quality and beauty and became differential in design (axe, spear, and knife) for the performance of special jobs. Subsequently Palaeolithic man added bones, horns, and ivory to the list of raw materials for tools and weapons. He caught fish with hook and line, used the dog in the chase, employed rotary motion for drilling holes even in stone, utilized the principle of the lever and fulcrum for moving heavy objects, and invented the bow and arrow, the first composite mechanism made by human kind.

Yet the development of these tools and weapons made possible the accumulation of but a very small surplus, probably just enough to provide minimum human needs during the unproductive months of the year. They did not lead to any extensive division of labour, to any important trade, or to any residual body of aesthetic works. When men moved, as they frequently did, they could carry their belongings on their backs or draw them on sledges. Yet, in spite of the low level of accomplishment, one very important ideology became established in many societies —man wanted to increase his control over his physical environment so that he would not suffer from want. This desire is clear from improvements in techniques and from the character of supplications to supernatural powers. In nearly all primitive religions there are prayers, rites, spells, and incantations to the totem to make the hunting good or to assist the supplicant one way or another in overcoming some material difficulty.[2]

About 10,000 years ago important changes took place which were to lead to the creation of economic surplus and to the achievement of higher levels of civilisation. With the melting of the northern ice sheets at the end of the last glacial period, the steppes and tundras of Europe were transformed into temperate forests and the prairies south of the Mediterranean and in Hither Asia were converted into deserts with oases. Consequently hunting in these areas became poorer, and man sought a new way to provide himself with sustenance. In the solution of his problem he effected one of the major technological revolutions in history —the domestication of grains and animals. This agricultural revolution came with the beginning of a new age in history—the New Stone or Neolithic Age.[3]

Probably the first grains to be sown and harvested for human

3

food were related to wheat and barley; and they were selected from a number of wild plant seeds and tubers that had been gathered by Palaeolithic man in his quest for food. To wheat and barley were added in various places rice, millet, Indian corn or maize, yams, manioc, and squash. The first animals to be brought under control, cared for, and used to aid in the chase or to supplement its rewards were dogs, sheep, goats, cattle, and pigs. They were chosen either because they had not fled to the north like the reindeer, because they were relatively docile, or because they were particularly productive of the things men wanted.

The domestication of plants and animals had far-reaching effects. Tools were improved and further differentiated. Polishing of stone was more generally resorted to in order to get a finer edge for harvesting grain, cutting wood, and slaughtering animals. The hoe and sickle, the polished stone axe, and better knives bear testimony of the trend. The cultivation of plant crops involved new problems of food storage and led to the creation of the earthen pot, which was far superior for this purpose to bags of skins, horns, or woven baskets. Fermentation was discovered, which allowed Neolithic man to make beverages with which to enliven festive occasions or to relieve the boredom of rainy days. Spinning and weaving were developed, which made possible a substitute for animal skins as clothing. And bodily decoration with shells and beads, which indicated the existence of aesthetic considerations, became more common.

As can readily be imagined, the new agricultural technology placed a premium upon readily arable and fertile land. Oases and naturally drained marsh areas along rivers or around lakes were probably the most desirable, for there few if any trees had to be cleared away. In such areas caves did not exist, so man began to turn to other types of housing—to tents made from hides, to shelters from branches or grass, and to wooden or sod houses. Such structures made possible the establishment of villages of the fixed settlement type, which had the advantages of being convenient to the place of work, of facilitating social intercourse, of accumulating human aesthetic achievements and knowledge, and of providing protection. On the last score, the need was apparently very great, for in times of poor crops and threatened famine people migrated in search of greener pastures which, if need be, they would take by force. Then, too, people who lived on the periphery of settled communities preyed upon their neighbours. These nomadic and semi-nomadic people were for long a serious problem, for inasmuch as they lived as food gatherers and later as shepherds they had to contend with wild beasts and keep their fighting ability at a high level. They were the "barbarians" who invaded settled areas.

The technological revolution in the Age of Copper

Important as was settled agriculture as a foundation for the production of a surplus which would provide that leisure which man needs for intellectual and artistic pursuits, the Neolithic Age failed to meet some of the basic conditions of economic progress. It did not have sufficiently effective or specialized tools to permit much of a division of labour. It did not employ animal or mechanical power on a large enough scale to supplement human effort to a meaningful degree. It had only the beginnings of a social or political system which could organize the collective efforts of a group for effecting major capital improvements. And it did not have means of transportation adequate for the development of extensive commerce.

The Age of Copper, or, as it is more elaborately called, the Chalcolithic Age, marked an advance in most of these respects. It inaugurated a "technological revolution" during the 1,000 years prior to 3000 B.C. which was, in the opinion of many, more far-reaching in its consequences than any other prior to A.D. 1600. Improvements in techniques made possible important gains in production per capita and laid the foundation for an urban development that was essential to forward strides in intellectual and cultural endeavour.

The geographical area within which the technological revolution of the Copper Age took place is bounded on the west by the Sahara and the Mediterranean Sea, on the east by the Thar Desert and the Himalayas, on the north by the Balkan, Caucasus, Elburz, and Hindu Kush Mountains, and on the south by the Tropic of Cancer. It is a region in which a surplus has to be provided for non-productive seasons. It has fertile land around oases, along river valleys, and in mountain passes. It had the wild grapevine, dependable crops of dates, figs, and olives with which man could supplement his cultivated crops. It had easily navigable waterways for commerce. It was comparatively well protected from mass migrations from outside. And it had relatively cloudless skies, which facilitated observation of the heavens —observation that led to the acquisition of knowledge useful in guiding the traveller on his way and in keeping track of the seasons.

Settled agriculture within this area was carried on most successfully near oases and along the Nile, at the mouth of the Tigris and Euphrates Rivers, and along the Indus River. Agricultural surpluses were exchanged along the rivers and with the wilder food gatherers on the fringes of settlement. Commerce of this kind made men familiar with new products turned out by their neighbours and whetted a demand for new utilitarian and luxury goods. Furthermore, problems of drainage and irrigation in river agriculture contributed to co-operative effort on a relatively large scale. Out of this experience came organization for the pooling of human resources, leadership in productive enterprise, some division of labour, and a recognition of the necessity of "investment" of present energies for the purpose of future gain. Gradually the desire for more products, the possibility of obtaining them in exchange for surplus agricultural goods, and the need for control over the use of water created a situation conducive to technological change.

As the reader has already assumed from the name of the age that we are examining, one of the major technological developments in this period consisted in the discovery and use of copper. This metal had obvious advantages over stone. It was less fragile, could be more easily repaired, took a better edge, made lighter and stronger tools, and could be more readily shaped by hammering or casting into a greater variety of products. Although it was not so universally distributed over the earth's surface as stone, its lightness and consequent ease of transport gave it a preferred position in areas, like the delta of the Tigris and Euphrates, which had no stone. Its cost was high, however, which restricted its use, especially in districts like Egypt where flint was readily available. Nevertheless, we find it being used among the Sumerians in the delta of the Tigris and Euphrates for tools, weapons, vessels, and seals with which to indicate the ownership of goods.

Probably the first copper was found in a relatively pure state in nature, but by 3000 B.C. the metal was being reduced from ore in furnaces fired with charcoal.[4] It was placed in crucibles that would withstand high temperatures; it was handled with tongs; and it was cast in moulds. The production of copper provided techniques essential to the manufacture of a large number of metals, and therefore it is not strange that we find silver, lead, and tin being produced by similar methods almost at once. And before long tin began to be added to copper to make bronze.

Important as were these technological advances in metallurgy, they were rivalled in significance by changes in ceramics. Pottery made from clay and fired to obtain greater durability was inherited from earlier times. Within the time-span under discussion Egyptians developed ways of glazing and decorating pottery to make the more durable and beautiful faïence. The inhabitants of Hither Asia invented the potter's wheel, which made possible extremely rapid manufacture of fine products of perfectly symmetrical design. The invention appears to have reached Egypt by 2700 B.C. and the Indus by 2500 B.C. The principle of the wheel was in itself of greatest moment, for it is essential in the transmission of power and in the reduction of friction. Wheeled vehicles were in use in Mesopotamia, for example, by 3000 B.C., in India before 2500 B.C., in Crete by 2000 B.C., in Egypt by 1600 B.C., and in China and Sweden by 1000 B.C. Curiously enough, they were never developed in the Maya, Inca, or Aztec civilisations, nor was the principle of the wheel used in them for anything except toys !

Among other technological developments mention should be made of the manufacture of brick, at first sun-dried but in India by 2500 B.C. fired in kilns. Wooden ploughs appeared in Egypt and Mesopotamia about 3000 B.C. and soon afterwards in India, although not in China until about 1400 B.C. Ploughs required animal power for efficient traction, and oxen were equipped with yokes that fitted on the broad shoulders or horns of the beast to pull them.

This union of livestock with the cultivation of crops meant not only the addition of animal energy to human energy in agriculture, but it also meant the production of more humus for the soil and the beginning of a new form of transportation. By 3000 B.C. camels and asses, or horses, were known to the people of Hither Asia and were gradually put to use by others, the horse having been introduced into Egypt between 1800 and 1600 B.C. Unfortunately, the collar for the horse, probably adopted from the ox yoke, was so constructed that it choked the animal when he pulled a heavy load.[5] For this reason and because the ass and horse were much smaller than now, they were not used as draught animals in ancient times except for light vehicles like chariots but were employed as pack and riding animals. It was not until the ninth or tenth century A.D. that the breastplate and later the collar were adjusted to fit on the shoulders of the horse rather than on his throat. For his part, the ox was not very efficient for transport, because he was slow; his load was limited by friction of the wheels on dirt roads; and his hoofs, like the horse's, wore out on hard surfaces. Not until the tenth century A.D. were iron shoes with nails used to overcome this last difficulty.[6]

Finally, the period of which we are speaking witnessed a considerable improvement in water transport. Although Neolithic men had at least rafts and canoes with which they made hazardous journeys, it was probably not until a little before 3000 B.C. that craft capable of carrying substantial cargoes were constructed and that the sail was used to propel them. The sail was a major invention, because it increased the productive efficiency of man by adding to his technology one of the earliest methods of harnessing inorganic energy—a source of power that was in modern times to revolutionize man's economic life.[7]

Technological advances of the Age of Copper had two major economic consequences—they helped bring about a greater amount of trade and a greater division of labour. The latter development is particularly clear in the case of coppersmiths, potters, and to a degree carpenters. The metallurgical process of refining and working copper required specialized knowledge, equipment, and concentration of activity, which took it out of the hands of farmers working at home. Coppersmiths devoted their labours almost exclusively to their craft. By restricting information about their skill to a limited number of apprentices, they retained for themselves enough of the market to keep themselves steadily employed. There is evidence that at least in the making of finished products many of the smiths were itinerants or were employed in noble or priestly households.

Similarly, the potter possessed a skill that was learned only with patience and practice, and he too was frequently an itinerant worker. He carried his wheel to suitable clay near a market, for that was easier than trying to transport finished and fragile products over long distances. Carpentry, masonry, and brick-making were somewhat less specialized, for farmers could perform in a rough way at least the major tasks of these crafts. As more elaborate tools came into use, as more refined products were demanded, and as the effective demand of the market became larger, a division of labour and a great increase in productivity per worker took place.

The growth of commerce is indicated by a variety of data. Inasmuch as the earliest centres of advanced civilisation (delta of the Tigris and Euphrates, the Nile Valley, and the Indus River area) had no copper deposits, it is clear that copper was imported by these areas. Incidentally it would appear that working copper and some of the other new techniques originated in mountainous areas and oases and were borrowed by districts with large agricultural surpluses. In any case, copper first used on the lower Tigris and Euphrates came from Oman on the Persian Gulf, while lead and silver were brought chiefly from the Taurus Mountains in Asia Minor. Copper came into Egypt from Mount Sinai at the northern end of the Red Sea and to the Indus River people from Rajputana and possibly Baluchistan. Similarly wood entered trade both for construction purposes and for charcoal, Egypt obtaining supplies from Syria through the port of Byblos, near the modern city of Beirut, and from Central Africa. Tin, which is not widely found, must have been carried long distances; and we know that Egypt obtained gold from Nubia to the south. Archaeologists have found finished Egyptian products in Sumer, and the products of Sumer and India, far from their place of origin. They believe, moreover, that the spread of such techniques as the potter's wheel indicates a far-flung, if not an intensive, commerce. Finally, a new development was taking place that would have been impossible without commerce—that was the establishment of cities. These new concentrations of population, which were to contribute so much to civilisation, were almost completely dependent upon trade for food and for industrial raw materials.

The urban revolution of the early Bronze Age

The first cities[8] of which we have record were established prior to 2500 B.C. in the three river valleys that have been mentioned as the earliest centres of advanced civilisation. Somewhat later, cities appeared in other river valleys, like that of the Yellow River in China, at places producing such goods as copper, and at commercial centres around the fringes or along trade routes between the earlier cultures. In all cases, it should be noted, the earliest cities came into being primarily for economic reasons. They were not essentially the creation of political systems to facilitate administration.

That the establishment of cities should be glorified by the term "urban revolution" requires a word by way of explanation. As was stated in Chapter I, cities have been the loci for the creation of the great intellectual and cultural works of man, and hence the establishment of urban centres is a significant part of our story. Second, these early cities witnessed an intensification of economic activity on a large scale, a greater concentration of capital than had ever before been known, the growth of new techniques of production and distribution, a division of labour, and the beginnings of such important economic institutions as money, banking, and a law of contracts. Third, these early cities developed writing and systems of numerical notation which made possible the ready communication of ideas and the accumulation of man's experience for the benefit of posterity.

The geographical environment in which the earliest cities appeared is so strikingly similar that it is worthy of closer examination. The delta of the Tigris and Euphrates Rivers, where the Sumerian culture developed, is an area about the size of Denmark. The soil there is alluvial and extremely fertile.[9] The marshy land had to be drained in order to be cultivated, which necessitated the combined efforts of many men. The rivers stretch through a broad and somewhat arid plain 600 miles from their headwaters in the Armenian plateau and empty into the Persian

Gulf, the country thus having water routes both inland and to neighbouring lands overseas. The plain was protected by deserts and mountains, but through these barriers were gaps which made the area more susceptible to attack than either Egypt or the Indus River region. In fact, an inordinate amount of the energy of the Tigris-Euphrates peoples was diverted to war, which accounts, in part, for their many contributions to the art of warfare and for the endless destruction of their accomplishments. Finally, the plain was too long to be consolidated successfully into a unit, and it developed into two major parts, Assyria to the north of the thirty-fourth parallel and Babylonia to the south.

The valley of the Nile, the home of Egyptian culture, is 550 miles in length from the Delta to the First Cataract but is extremely narrow above the Delta, averaging about 12 miles in width. It comprises an area less than that of modern Switzerland. The annual floods of the river had created a deep alluvial soil with many marshes. Here, too, land had to be reclaimed and floodwaters had to be controlled by drainage and irrigation— a task that was easier than in the Tigris-Euphrates because of the greater regularity of the inundations and their arrival well before the planting season. The Nile Valley was better protected by barren deserts than the Tigris-Euphrates Valley, yet it had equally good facilities for river transportation, and the river emptied into a sea that was easily navigable. It also had stone from the nearby edges of the valley, which the Tigris-Euphrates lacked, but it was equally poor in wood and minerals. Finally, its length is noteworthy; one of the recurring political problems in Egyptian history was how to knit all the valley together rather than to let it break into two major sections or, what was worse, into a multitude of noble states.

In India the earliest cities appeared prior to 2500 B.C. in the flood plains of the Indus River. Here good protection was afforded by deserts and mountains, and water transportation was made possible by the river and its five tributaries. Nor was the

Indian Ocean too formidable for the existing techniques of navigation, although it was more repelling than the mild and tideless Mediterranean or the Persian Gulf. Land to be fertile had to be properly watered, while minerals and timber had to be transported from afar.[10]

In places like these, then, rich in soil, made productive by a water supply that had to be controlled by man, poor in minerals and timber, which had to be imported, and provided with waterways that could be navigated, the earliest cities came into being. These urban agglomerations were not large by our standards, some having a population of perhaps 40,000, but they were considerably bigger than the agricultural villages that had preceded them. The fundamental techniques of production in them had not advanced much over those of the Age of Copper, except that bronze was supplanting copper as the chief metal, finer goods were being produced, and a greater division of labour was visible in such trades as baking, brewing, and building as a result of the concentrated market.

What impresses us most in these early cities is, however, the concentration of capital, in the broadest sense of the word. In Sumer this concentration was effected primarily by the temples, in Egypt by the Pharaohs, and in India probably by a bourgeois class. In Sumer, for which more complete information is available than for the other areas, the temples owned land which they leased to tenants; they granted advances (loans) of seed and implements to tillers of the soil in return for a charge which in essence was interest; they built and maintained drainage and irrigation ditches; they planned production; they employed craftsmen in their own shops and sold the goods thus produced; and they catered to those engaged in trade. From this activity they were able to amass a surplus which could be and was used for expanding production. They were not, however, responsible for the defence of the city, this task being left to the city governor or king.

In Egypt the situation seems to have been somewhat different. Here a political leader was the chief agent in the concentration of wealth, although he assumed god-like prerogatives which fortified his claim to ultimate ownership of land and to goods and services from the people. From payments made to him and from profits in the crafts in his extensive household economy, he accumulated great amounts of capital. A relatively large part of it seems to have been employed in non-productive activity, like the construction of elaborate tombs and the burial of wealth with the dead. The Great Pyramid, for example, constructed between 2420 and 2270 B.C., contains 2,300,000 stone blocks weighing an average of two and a half tons apiece and required, according to Herodotus, the labour of 100,000 men working over a twenty-year period. But some of the wealth of the Pharaohs was used to build canals and cities, to exploit the copper deposits at Sinai, to fit out trading expeditions, or to expand production in the royal workshops.

With the appearance of cities, the concentration of capital, a greater division of labour, and increased trade, money came into being. Money, which may be defined as a medium of exchange, a store of wealth, and a measure of value, albeit a fluctuating one, was in the form of metals (gold, silver, or copper) which were weighed out at each transaction. Subsequently bars of metal had the amount of their contents stamped on them. Only much later (*circa* 700 B.C.) were pieces of metal (coins) of fixed weight and fineness issued and guaranteed by political states. Money, although used in a limited degree in this period, was a tremendous convenience, for goods could readily be exchanged for it. Under a system of barter a person with goods to exchange must find someone who has goods that he wants and who wants what he has—an operation that is at best cumbersome. Because money was a boon to trade, it deepened and widened the division of labour. It also facilitated the amassing of surplus, or capital formation, for it could be stored more easily and with less deterioration than, let us say, wheat. Finally it could be brought together from many more sources than could real products, because it was easier to transport, and hence aided in tapping the savings of more people.

Urban development was also accompanied by several other new business practices. We have already mentioned the beginnings of the institution of credit and interest-taking in Sumer— a practice that was to become of the utmost importance in economic development because it provided a way of placing capital in the hands of enterprising persons. We have likewise referred to the seal as a means of indicating the ownership of goods, which by its increased use seems to show a growth in the principle of private property. In this period, too, a law of contracts, which recognized the binding force of business agreements, came into being. This law was written into early codes, like the Code of Hammurabi[11] shortly after 1750 B.C., and became a generally accepted concept in business procedure. Employing and employed classes became more clearly delineated, and with them there appeared the wage system. In fact, many of the aspects of modern economic institutions, at least in embryonic form, seem to have been present in the early cities.

The question now remains, did the more adequate combining of many of what we have called factors of economic progress actually result in a larger production of goods and services per capita ? Of course we have no direct statistical data as a basis for a firm reply, but all the circumstantial evidence indicates that the answer should be in the affirmative. The cities seem to have brought with them a higher standard of living. People were better housed in the brick and stone buildings than they had been previously in mud and reed huts. In some places there are indications of organized sewage disposal and water supply. City granaries held stores of food which could be, and were, used to alleviate local famines, and the upper classes enjoyed luxuries in greater abundance than ever before. Finally, there was an increase in population, which, so long as there is no diminution of goods per capita, is an indication of economic progress.

To be sure, there were germs of decay within the economy of the urban areas. Wages were too low or too much in the form of goods that had to be consumed at once to permit the development of an ever-expanding market. Wealth was concentrated in the hands of priests, kings, nobles, or traders who had put much of their surplus into non-productive things, like religious worship, rather than into efforts that would have increased goods available for consumption. Finally, population reached a size at which existing techniques, resources, capital, and trade were unable to provide a further increase in goods and services per capita. While cities were growing, however, there appears to have been greater surpluses than previously for cultural and intellectual activity.

Revolutions in knowledge and culture

The establishment of cities did, in fact, contribute to a "revolution in knowledge" and to a "revolution in culture." The former was of particular importance and may be classed along with fire, the invention of money, and the use of inorganic energy as one of the epoch-making events in man's past.

In the most primitive state of *homo sapiens*, little emphasis is to be placed on the adjective *sapiens*. Man undoubtedly acquired knowledge by simple trial-and-error methods. In learning to smelt copper ore, for example, he probably got copper accidentally, but then, to get more, he endeavoured to reproduce the conditions that gave the original result without knowing precisely what the essential conditions were. After many attempts, in which earth with no metallic content was undoubtedly heated many times, man learned that only one kind of earth, that is, copper ore, would produce the desired metal. This "rule of thumb" he passed on to his successors, who followed it slavishly without knowing what actually happened in the process of smelting. The "revolution in knowledge" occurred when man began to understand and was able to explain *why* one event followed another—when man could tell what the result would be if certain conditions were given. This is the essence of science—the ordering of demonstrable or observable data to explain a sequence of events.

The development of science from mere rules of thumb has had an enormous impact on the history of man, especially in that it has given him a greater control over his environment and has allowed him to plan for that control. But the establishment of the scientific ideal has been a long-drawn-out process and is not universally established even today, impeded as it has been by superstition, tradition, false concepts, and vested interests. Consequently a full-blown and generally accepted scientific attitude was not to be expected at the early date of the urban revolution. What happened then was that certain tools necessary for scientific development were created, and meagre beginnings in the ordering of demonstrable and observable data were made.

The chief tools invented were writing, simplified systems of numerical notation, and systems of weights and measures. Significantly enough, each one of these tools was developed from economic activity. In Sumer, for example, temple priests who managed elaborate business undertakings needed a way of keeping records that would be intelligible to their successors as well as to people with whom they dealt. The earliest form of writing was, as has been previously stated, in book-keeping and consisted of symbols that had an agreed upon meaning. These first symbols were easily understood pictures, or pictograms. In time these were abbreviated so that they were conventional signs (hieroglyphs) and were supplemented by symbols for ideas (ideograms) which could not be easily rendered pictorially.

Then in Sumer, at least, another step was taken which was to give a sound value to things and ideas and to render the sound value by a phonetic symbol, or phonogram. This last development made easier the adoption of an alphabet, which appeared in a

Semitic language in the nineteenth century B.C. Similarly a system of numerical notation was simply the adoption of symbols in place of a collection of grouped lines on a tally stick. Thus in Sumer, while numbers 1 to 9 were expressed by straight lines, 10 was expressed by a circle, 20 by two circles, etc. (a decimal system), except in counting the volume of certain things like beer, where a semicircle stood for 60, two semicircles for 120, etc. (a sexagesimal system).

Concomitantly with these developments more attention was given to generally agreed upon weights and measures. A man building his own reed hut could measure his materials according to the size of his hands or the length of his arm and be accurate enough for his purposes. But a corps of specialized workers building an elaborate temple could not rely upon such haphazard methods, for a beam resting on two pillars had to fit more exactly than would have been possible if each workman did his measuring with his own anatomy. Similarly, in trade it was necessary to have generally agreed upon measures and weights (to be used in a balance) for all transactions involving the transfer of goods.

Certain elementary principles of mathematics, probably the oldest of the sciences, came directly out of economic activity. Thus we find Sumerians using multiplication and multiplication tables in various activities. They multiplied length x breadth in order to determine the size of a field, and length x breadth x height to get the volume of a stack of bricks; and they could explain *why* these procedures *always* gave the right answer. They used fractions, and the Egyptians had a formula which gave the correct value to π. The latter were particularly adept at the geometry necessary for constructing buildings connected with their funerary cult. They knew how to determine the angle of slope of a pyramid and were able to execute their plans so exactly that in the case of the Great Pyramid the sides of approximately 755 feet have a mean error of only a little over half an inch.

Even the beginnings of astronomy were closely connected

with economic needs. From celestial observation it was learned that the position of the heavenly bodies could measure the passage of time, tell the seasons of the year, and indicate the points of the compass. As a result calendars were developed by which the businessman could decide when a contract should be executed and the farmer could determine when to prepare for floods or when to plant. Similarly, diagrams were constructed by which the traveller could find his way across the trackless desert or the sailor his route when out of sight of land. The Sumerians developed a lunar calendar and the Egyptians, a solar one—the lineal ancestor of our own. The latter people divided the year at first into 365 days but came to realize from further observation that the seasonal year is approximately $365\frac{1}{4}$ days. In the invention of apparatus for keeping track of shorter spaces of time, the exigencies of economic life seem likewise to have played a role, for the businessman needed to "know the time" in order to make and keep appointments, and working-men engaged upon a co-operative task had to have a measure of time to determine when to begin their labours. To meet these requirements, the Sumerians divided the day into twelve double hours, which has given us our twenty-four hour day, the week into seven days, and the year into twelve months. Both they and the Egyptians employed sun dials, movements of the stars, or water clocks, which worked on the principle of the hour-glass, for regularizing the activities of life.

In addition to these achievements, there were many others. Some knowledge of the effects of drugs was learned, although medicine was retarded by beliefs in the healing powers of chants and incantations. Surgery made greater strides forward, for, if a stone rolled on a working-man's leg and broke it, the cause of the injury and the need for remedial action minimized recourse to magic cures. Moreover, the Egyptians learned something of human anatomy from the practice of mummification, which involved the removal of the viscera. They were able to set broken bones, to hold them in place with splints, to bandage wounds, and to perform certain operations. In engineering, they employed the inclined plane, the water level, and the square. And they were expert enough to build dams and gates whereby they reclaimed land from the Faiyum, which was below sea level, and at the same time provided storage for flood-water that could be released for irrigation in the dry season.

From what has preceded it is clear that in both Sumer and Egypt a beginning was made in the collection of observable and demonstrable data and that some effort was expended in organizing in sequential order those data pertaining particularly to practical questions. Perhaps most of the findings should be classed as "rules of thumb," but in some instances, as in geometry, attempts were made to provide "proofs" that would explain why given conditions always gave the same results. In any case, writing and the use of writing materials, which by comparison with the flimsy paper of today gave great permanency and perhaps imparted to authors an added sense of responsibility, made possible the preservation of data for the analytical scrutiny of generations yet to come.[12]

With the urban revolution there were what have generally been recognized by historians as advances in the arts. The mud-brick temples of Sumer had an austere, if somewhat ponderous, beauty, while Sumerian sculpture, although failing to elicit the admiration of all modern critics, was at least an attempt to render human forms—gods, city governors, and priests—in a realistic manner. In Egypt architecture reflected more refinement, with the fluted columns (copied in stone from the bundles of papyrus reeds which had previously been used as pillars) arranged in colonnades of great beauty. Egyptian sculpture connected with funerary rites is held in high esteem. Paintings in tombs, representing the life on the deceased's estate, are fine in line, show a search for a solution of perspective and are bright if monotonous in colour. Even in music, these early urban centres made a contribution, for they assembled drums, flutes, horns, and harps, formed melodies, and employed, if they did not invent, the heptatonic (seven-note) scale. In brief the arts reflect greater refinement, more precise workmanship, and a more extensive development than had been apparent in previous ages.

Thus from Palaeolithic times, some half a million years ago, to approximately 2700 B.C., men in a few selected places had definitely moved in the direction of what we in Western culture consider civilisation. They had improved their techniques of making a living to the point where surplus was available to permit the creation and enjoyment of the "finer things of life." They had displayed an interest in the collection and ordering of observable data—one of the greatest of intellectual pursuits. And they had created works of art that even by our own standards have aesthetic value.

FOOTNOTES TO CHAPTER II

1 Arnold J. Toynbee in *The Study of History* presents a list of twenty-one cultures which presumably were the major cultures of all time. Once he introduces a culture like the Eskimo to his list, he invalidates its selectivity, for many cultures can be found that equal the Eskimo in every respect.

2 Knowledge of Palaeolithic civilisation comes mainly from archaeology and anthropology. The former endeavours to reconstruct the story from remains of man's activity. The latter relies more upon comparative studies of groups now living in primitive conditions. Examples of people at the Palaeolithic stage have been found in central Africa and in the jungles of Malaya. See V. Gordon Childe, *Man Makes Himself*, C. A. Watts & Co. Ltd., London, 1941 and *What Happened in History*, Penguin Books, Inc., New York, 1946; G. Renard, *Life and Work in Prehistoric Times*, Alfred A. Knopf, Inc., New York, 1929, and G. P. Murdock, *Our Primitive Contemporaries*, The Macmillan Company, New York, 1934.

3 The Neolithic Age cannot be given terminal dates for all parts of the world. Neolithic civilisation has persisted in certain areas down to the present. The North American Indian had a Neolithic culture when the first white settlers arrived on these shores.

4 Bellows to produce a forced draft did not come into use until 1500 B.C.

5 Richard Lefebvre des Noëttes, *L'Attelage et le cheval de selle à travers les âges*, Picard, Paris, 1931, 2 vols., and *La force motrice animale à travers*

les âges, Berger-Levrault, Paris, 1924. Modern experiments with the ancient harness indicate that the horse could pull only about half a ton.

6 Romans had a horse-shoe which was tied to the hoof. Probably it was not very efficient.

7 Gravitation, an inorganic source of power, had been used previously to assist in rolling or sliding materials down-hill and in carrying a floating vessel down-stream.

The water-wheel was not invented until near the end of the first millennium B.C.

8 A city may be defined as "a function of the concentration of population in such a manner that the greater the density and the greater the population and the continuous area exhibiting this density, the more of a city it is."

9 Documents of about 2500 B.C. attest to an extraordinarily high return of barley.

10 Similar conditions were found in the early civilised parts of China on the Yellow River. Two major differences were the open country to the north through which invaders might come and the outlet of the rivers into the Pacific Ocean, a body of water so vast that with existing techniques of navigation the Chinese were not able to use it as an artery of commerce to distant lands.

11 See below, p. 68.

12 Sumerians wrote on clay tablets, pressing out their characters with reeds. The characters were usually of wedge shape or cuneiform. Egyptians wrote on papyrus reeds pressed together to form a smooth paper-like mat.

FOR FURTHER READING

Gordon Childe, *Man Makes Himself* (1941)
———— *What Happened in History* (1946)
F. M. Feldhaus, *Technik der Vorzeit* (1914)
G. P. Murdock, *Our Primitive Contemporaries* (1939)
G. Renard, *Life and Work in Prehistoric Times* (1929)
M. Rostovtzeff, *A History of the Ancient World*, Vol. I (1926)
Ralph Turner, *The Great Cultural Traditions* (1941), 2 Vols.

III

EMPIRE CULTURES
OF THE BRONZE AGE

FROM THE THIRD TO THE FIRST
MILLENNIUM B.C.

From approximately the third to the first millennium B.C., Hither Asia, the Nile Valley, and the region of the Aegean Sea passed from the Age of Copper through the Age of Bronze to the Age of Iron. In these areas, which had experienced the agrarian, technological, and urban revolutions of the preceding period, great empires were formed, each with a distinctive culture. During the Age of Bronze these empire cultures attained, in comparison with other cultures, their highest levels of civilisation; then in the first millennium B.C. they bowed before the superiority of Hellas and adopted much of Greek culture as their own.

Economic progress and war

Prior to the attainment of their peaks of civilisation, these ancient empires achieved considerable economic progress. This they did without advances in techniques comparable to those of the thousand years prior to 3000 B.C. In fact, the only technological innovations in the millennium and a half from 2700 to 1200 B.C. worth mentioning here were the development of bronze as a substitute for copper, the use of larger ships equipped with the rudder, the making of clear glass in Egypt,[1] and the smelting of iron, which inaugurated the next period. Most economic progress seems to have come from an extension of trade, a greater division of labour, and a deepening of investment. The expansion of commerce increased the supply of natural resources by opening up formerly isolated or undeveloped territories, and it permitted various areas to concentrate on the production of those goods in which they had comparative advantages. Labour became more specialized as commerce was extended, as the size of business operations was enlarged, and as economic goods became more complex. Investment per worker increased, and the craftsman at the end of the Bronze Age had more and better tools than his counterpart of the Age of Copper. Finally, better political organization provided greater security for economic activity and made large-scale undertakings possible.

In the Bronze Age, however, several forces were at work which tended to hinder the functioning of the positive factors of economic progress. Wealth was used unproductively; labour did not provide an expanding market; and population increases resulted in a pressure of people upon the means of subsistence. At least the end of the Bronze Age was marked by mass migrations of many peoples, presumably impelled to move by a need for food.

A decline in economic well-being with a culture was, moreover, frequently accompanied by internal troubles and by attacks from other cultures. In fact, from the beginning of written records, war looms large as a phase of human activity and as a cause of shifts in centres of power and civilisation. What often happened was that some backward area would borrow techniques and technology from an advanced culture, just as Russia and Japan have done in recent times, and employ them to develop their own economies and military power. In cases where resources, organizing ability, and the will to succeed were great, backward areas were able to conquer more highly civilised regions and to alter drastically, if not destroy, the older culture.

So often did this happen between 2700 and 1200 B.C. that we cannot refrain from reflecting upon the relation of war to great civilising achievements. From the history of this period it is clear that a distinction must be made between wars that have been overwhelmingly destructive of material well-being and of civilisation and those that have made possible a greater exploitation of nature's resources and a spread of civilised cultures. Second, advanced cultures have seldom taken the precautions necessary to prevent the diffusion of their military techniques and weapons to backward areas and thus to preserve advantages that were the foundation of their superiority. Third, it is remarkable that so-called backward areas have so frequently defeated more civilised areas because of some particular military ascendancy in strategy, tactics, logistics, or morale. Finally, it is worth mentioning that those cultures which looked to war—to preying on others—as a fundamental ideology and as a way of sustaining themselves did not achieve such high levels of civilisation as more peaceful cultures. They devoted too large a proportion of their energies to destructive rather than to constructive ends.

Rises and falls of civilisation in Egypt

Of all the empire cultures of the Bronze Age that of Egypt permits one of the most instructive case studies of factors that determine *degrees* of civilisation. Not only did Egyptian culture have a recorded existence of over three millenniums in which basic ideologies and art forms were amazingly stable, but it experienced rises and falls in its level of civilisation which were so regular that they seem almost rhythmic. Furthermore, data regarding Egypt are adequate enough to allow the making of general statements concerning those forces that contributed to the shifting stages of artistic and intellectual achievement and of control over human and physical environment.

The first appreciable economic surplus in Egypt of which we know was amassed as a result of the agricultural, technological, and urban revolutions described in the last chapter. In the course of time, however, this surplus was greatly increased and, in part, as a result of what were fundamentally political forces. As a late tradition has it,[2] one of the many local lords of the land succeeded in bringing Upper and Lower Egypt together in 3200 B.C., and his successors maintained their supremacy and enforced peace until 2270 B.C. This long period of law and order permitted an inordinate amount of human energy to be devoted to economic and cultural ends. Furthermore, centralized authority led to an organization of effort that produced economic results far beyond what could have been realized by the dispersed efforts of individuals.

The Pharaohs of Egypt played, indeed, an exceptionally important role in the economic life of their country. The earliest of them in the formative period of Egyptian culture had claimed that they were divine and were entitled to special rights, privileges, and prerogatives. Such claims, which are frequent in the pages of history, were successfully maintained and in time became established as institutions. They gave the Pharaohs rights to an individual's immortal soul, to all the goods and services of a subject, and to ownership of all the land of the kingdom. On the basis of such principles the rulers of Egypt demanded revenues and offerings from their subjects and in the course of time amassed great fortunes. The Pharaohs along with officials and priests constituted a wealthy group which determined the "investment policy" of Egypt. Some of their resources they put into manufacturing, most of Egypt's industrial output coming from lordly household establishments, and some went into foreign commerce over which the Pharaohs had a virtual monopoly.

With the growth of industry, there was an increase in the division of labour. Crafts became differentiated, and it became possible to distinguish smiths, carpenters, stone-masons, jewellers, and the like. Obviously the construction of anything so vast and intricate as a temple or a pyramid necessitated the employment of all kinds of specialists from ox drivers to skilled architects. Moreover, tasks within crafts became specialized, pictures taken from tombs showing different workmen combining their separate

Mediterranean Sea

Sais

Tanis

Heliopolis
Memphis

Faiyum

NILE R.

SINAI PENINSULA

Gulf of Suez

DESERT

Amarna

DESERT

Red Sea

Abydos

Karnak
Thebes
Luxor

Dead Sea

EGYPT

MILES

0   50   100

efforts in turning out standardized products like pots. Then with the development of foreign commerce, Egyptians began to draw upon the resources of other areas for materials that were not available at home. A few of these goods were obtained by conquest, as in the case of copper from the nearby mines of Mount Sinai, but most were procured through normal channels of trade. Thus Egypt received timber from Byblos in Syria, gold from Nubia to the south, perfumes and spices from Arabia, and lapis lazuli and other gems from Arabia.

Under conditions of unification and internal peace, of wealth in the hands of lords and kings, of increased investments in industry and commerce, and of a growth in the division of labour, Egypt enjoyed a period of relatively great economic well-being, especially during the Third, Fourth, and Fifth Dynasties, that is, from 2780 to 2420 B.C. Probably the over-all growth in population was not great enough to make the ancient Egyptians wonder, as Thomas Malthus did some four and a half millenniums later, if the goal of human-kind was to improve the economic condition of a given number of men or merely to increase the number of men on earth. All that we can say with certainty is that Egypt had enough production per capita to make possible a considerable concentration of economic surplus.

During this period Egypt attained one of its highest peaks of civilisation. Political and religious organisation, or control over human environment, was such as to provide individuals with a considerable degree of physical security; control over physical environment was sufficient to permit a relatively high degree of certainty that one would have the necessities of life; and leisure was adequate to allow the development of both the sciences and the arts. As we saw in the last chapter, Egyptians devised a solar calendar about this time, constructed a form of writing and numerical notation, and brought their science of mathematics to a point where they could erect with very little error such difficult buildings as pyramids.

In the arts, also, concepts of what to render in inanimate form, methods of work, and styles became differentiated and established. Belief in a physical life after death and the need for providing at least pictorially for a post-mortem existence gave rise to a search for a realistic portrayal of earthly things. Yet a lack of knowledge of perspective and of colour made a compromise with realism necessary; and this was done by a stylized representation of actual forms. So firmly were art styles of the Third, Fourth, and Fifth Dynasties established that they persisted without great change to Greek times. Moreover, artists had unusual opportunities to use their talents, for economic surplus and the elevated position of the Pharaohs and their officials made possible the construction of extravagant tombs and temples. These edifices represent in the opinion of most scholars one of the highest, if not the highest, attainment in Egyptian art.[3]

For many reasons the happy state of affairs that characterized the years from 2780 to 2420 B.C. did not continue. Not enough surplus was put into investments of those things that would have helped to increase production to keep pace with an expanding population. An extraordinary amount of wealth went into the construction of temples and tombs, and much was buried with the dead, although it was frequently put back in circulation by robbers. In brief, Egypt failed to maintain that nice balance in the use of surplus which would have resulted in an expansion both of goods and services per capita and of cultural accomplishments. The Pharaohs insisted, for example, upon using so much labour for ostentatious display that they failed to perform satisfactorily such mundane tasks as irrigating and draining the land or maintaining foreign commerce. Then, to make matters worse, religious restrictions curbed the search for new knowledge, and widespread rigidities in society stifled artistic expression. School instruction became stereotyped, as it so often does, was divorced from the real world and lauded the virtues of "traditional truths."

Finally, households of the lords became more economically self-sufficient and independent, and their heads became more reluctant to surrender goods and services to the king or otherwise to recognize his rule. From approximately 2400 B.C. the authority of the Pharaohs began to wane, and by 2270 B.C. the *nomes*, or small political units based on villages, became autonomous.

During the ensuing three centuries Egypt underwent a political, economic, and cultural dark age. Rivalry among the lords led to incessant local warfare. Lack of a strong central government prevented the undertaking of important land-reclamation projects, made difficult a rational utilization of the waters of the Nile, deprived the country of a force for protecting its frontiers, upset the most extensive manufacturing establishment—the household of the Pharaohs—and disrupted the conduct of both foreign and domestic commerce. Available evidence indicates clearly that economic production deteriorated during this period, and little has remained to give proof of anything but cultural decline. Yet techniques of production were kept alive in the household economy of the lords; astronomical lore appeared on coffin lids so that the deceased could keep track of time; embalming, and incidentally an interest in anatomy, were maintained; and private persons, because of the lack of economic centralization, began to engage in trade and manufacturing on their own account.

By about 2000 B.C. the Counts of Thebes managed by war and diplomacy to overcome the anarchy of the preceding years and to unite Egypt once again in a single state.[4] The re-establishment of a well-ordered, centralized government inaugurated a period of prosperity which lasted for over 200 years. Once again surplus was employed in long-range improvements, like irrigation projects and drainage in the Faiyum. Household manufacturing was revived and extended. Foreign commerce was restored with Syria, Palestine, Cyprus, Crete, and the Red Sea area. The use of money as a means of exchanging goods was more widely developed, and with it there was a greater division of labour, more private business for profit, and a development of business law. Foreign wars were few, and those in which Egypt was involved were not exhaustive and were easily won. Semitic tribes, which had penetrated the Delta in the previous period, were expelled, and Nubians to the south, who had frequently invaded Egypt in the past, were punished and were kept out by a series of fortresses at the First Cataract of the Nile.

All the evidence that we have indicates that, as economic activity was intensified in this period of the Twelfth Dynasty, conditions were again propitious for amassing surplus which could be devoted to the arts and sciences. It was then that the famous Labyrinth was constructed near the Faiyum reservoir—a series of buildings that covered an area of nearly a million square feet. Tombs, temples, and obelisks regained their earlier splendour. Jewellery, like that from the tombs in Memphis, was of excellent workmanship and composition, as were also painting and sculpture. This period marked the development of the earliest-known literature of a fictional and non-religious character. Poetry and prose, which frequently dealt with the preceding time of trouble when emotions ran high, enjoy the distinction of being regarded as the classics of Egyptian literature.

The years, then, from about 2000 to 1788 B.C. were a time when control over human and physical environment was favourable to individual security, to economic well-being, and to artistic achievement. As previously, however, the relatively high state of civilisation that was attained came to an end as a result of the lords becoming independent and of ensuing political and economic disintegration. As has so frequently happened in history, foreigners took advantage of unstable conditions to invade a comparatively wealthy area. In this case the newcomers were nomads of inferior civilisation—the Hyksos, or Shepherd Kings, who were probably Syrians led by Hittites and Aegeans. In any event they had apparently learned much about Egypt through commerce and had acquired some Egyptian techniques. In military affairs they had distinct advantages over the Egyptians, for not only were they able to consolidate their forces of war, but they employed the horse and light chariot which gave them superior mobility. Yet the Hyksos, although they overran the Nile Valley without great difficulty, were not successful in consolidating their conquests. In fact, they never succeeded in controlling their subjects effectively, and their supremacy was marked by anarchy and Egypt's second dark age.

From the Hyksos the Egyptians did, however, learn something. First, they acquired from their conquerors the horse and the chariot, the latter being the first wheeled vehicle on the banks of the Nile, and second, they had impressed upon their minds more strongly than ever before the economic advantages of political unification and order. Thus a movement was begun to oust the foreign overlords, and by about 1500 B.C. the Count of Thebes succeeded in mastering the Hyksos and once more in unifying the country. The Pharaohs of the succeeding dynasty, the Eighteenth (1580–1350 B.C.), were not, however, satisfied with the mere freeing of their country or with political unification. They had visions of grandeur that involved foreign conquests— an idea that they may have taken from the Hyksos' book of statecraft. At first, to be sure, the Egyptians concentrated upon a defence of their frontiers in order to prevent further invasions from Asia, but gradually their campaigns lost the aspect of punitive expeditions against recalcitrant neighbours and became wars of conquest. Palestine, Syria, Phoenicia, Cyprus, the territory of the Euphrates, and Nubia were subjugated and made to pay tribute to the homeland.[5]

For a time, conquest seems to have been a profitable enterprise for Egypt, with the spoils of war adding notably to the economic surplus of the country and with trade following the flags of the victorious armies. An inflow of precious metals and the need for a satisfactory medium of exchange for expanding commercial activity gave rise to a wider use of money and incidentally to a greater division of labour. Laws were further developed to provide more adequate rules for the conduct of business affairs; and the transfer of property, an essential element in economic progress, became more common, even land with its peasants and slaves changing hands with greater facility than hitherto. In fact, Egypt experienced a new wave of economic expansion, and its people enjoyed relative prosperity.

This economic revival of the Eighteenth Dynasty, like the previous ones, was accompanied by a cultural renaissance. Although this re-awakening is not considered to have attained a height of achievement commensurate with that of the Third, Fourth, and Fifth Dynasties, or with that of the Twelfth Dynasty, it was during this period of the Great Egyptian Empire that beautiful, if colossal, structures were built, like the Great Temple of Luxor with its famous avenue, which had no rival in the ancient world, the Temple of Amen-Ra at Karnak (the modern name for Thebes), the Temples of Deir-el-Bahari, and the buildings in the new capital at Tell-el-Amarna. Moreover, in the 200 years from 1580 to 1350 B.C. portrait statues of the Pharaohs displayed refinement and individuality; painting remained of high quality, although it showed signs of Eastern influence and of becoming over-ornate and even gaudy; tombs, like that of Tutankhamen, continued to be furnished lavishly; and literature flourished once more.

Towards the close of the Eighteenth Dynasty (1350 B.C.) and the end of the Bronze Age signs of Egypt's decline were in evidence. To maintain its supremacy in the foreign parts of the Great Empire, Egypt spent its resources lavishly on campaigns and fleets. Neither diplomacy, subsidies, nor dynastic marriages were able to arrest the endless troubles, frequently fomented by the Hittites and Assyrians, whom the Egyptians were unable completely to subdue. To make matters worse, the diversion of the country's energies into less and less profitable wars tended to reduce goods and services available to an enlarged population, while mercenaries returning from foreign conflicts often indulged their bellicose arts at home. Then an attempt to establish a single god for the whole world[6] ran foul of regional attachments to local gods and almost precipitated civil war in Egypt itself. With the large-scale migrations of the "People of the Sea" about 1200 B.C., which included migrations from the eastern Adriatic which pushed the people of Hellas east and southward, Egypt lost its foreign holdings, was invaded, and was torn by civil strife.

Subsequently the country was over-run by Nubians from the south, and still later it became an Assyrian province. Although during the Twenty-sixth Dynasty (663–609 B.C.) Egypt regained its independence, and endeavoured to restore the boundaries of the Great Empire, and enjoyed a brief economic and cultural renaissance—the Saitic Revival—the days of its greatest glory were past. Egypt came under Persian domination in 525 B.C., was conquered by Alexander the Great in 332 B.C., and finally became a Roman possession in 30 B.C.

Civilisation in the cultures of Mesopotamia

Not only along the Nile but also along the Tigris and Euphrates high levels of civilisation were attained during the Bronze Age. Here, as was seen in the last chapter, the agrarian, technological, and urban revolutions of the Age of Copper had made an impact and had inaugurated a movement that resulted in the creation of economic surplus. And this economic surplus had accompanied the extension of knowledge of the physical world, of greater control over that world, and of the beginning of writing and numerical notation. In the ensuing two millenniums further economic expansion took place, which again permitted greater civilising achievements. This expansion did not result from technical innovations. On the contrary it is to be accounted for by the extension of the use of existing techniques, by the establishing of political organization for the maintenance of order, and by the expansion of commerce.

MESOPOTAMIA

MILES

0   50   100

palacios

The development of trade was particularly essential in the economic development of the Tigris and Euphrates area, for the only important natural resource of the plain was mud. Although it produced lush crops, bricks, cooking utensils, and clay tablets it could not meet the demands for copper, tin, stone, and timber. The search for these things led to political unification, to a division of labour, and to the spread of the techniques of the dominant culture to neighbouring peoples. In the course of time these peoples were to attack their erstwhile teachers and to conquer them.

The earliest culture in Mesopotamia of which we know was that of Sumer near the mouths of the rivers. From it were diffused the ideologies, knowledge, styles of art, and other parts of transmissible learning to a district known as Akkad. Within the areas of Sumer and Akkad independent cities grew up, but gradually they were united to form two kingdoms. Then between 2500 and 2425 B.C. a famous ruler of Akkad, Sargon I, and his illustrious grandson, Naram-Sin, embarked on a policy of conquest. Thanks to superior military organization and equipment, which included the phalanx, the donkey, the chariot, and perhaps the horse, these kings had mobility and striking power beyond that of their enemies. Thus they were able to conquer Sumer, Assyria on the central Tigris, Elam to the east, and Syria on the Mediterranean, and even to conduct campaigns to Cyprus and to the shores of the Black Sea. From their foreign subjects they extracted tribute and with them, as well as with the people in Oman, Arabia, and the Bahrein Islands, they carried on trade. Thus they amassed wealth which inaugurated a golden age of lower Mesopotamian culture.

Soon, however, conditions became less propitious for economic and cultural growth. Less civilised peoples acquired the arts of war practised by the Akkadians and Sumerians and turned them against the conquerors. About 2400 B.C. a barbarian tribe from Gutium, east of the central Tigris, attacked the Empire, which had been built by Sargon, and obtained dominion over it. Now the direction of the flow of tribute was reversed; commerce languished; and household and temple industry declined. Then there followed a brief dark age, about contemporary with the first dark age in Egypt, in which no important contributions were made to civilisation.

Towards the end of the twenty-fourth century B.C. the people of Sumer and Akkad succeeded in expelling the invaders and in reconstituting much of Sargon's empire. In this period and in the twenty-third century B.C. an economic revival took place which was contemporary with the apogee of Sumer's cultural achievements. There was great activity in the collection of data regarding natural phenomena, especially in astronomy, and in mathematics. Architecture also flourished, and many of the great brick structures which were characterized by an unrelieved massiveness and by high towers or ziggurats[7] were constructed. Painting was not extensive, probably because the religion of the Sumerians and the Akkadians prescribed a future life of darkness that could not be rendered pictorially, but sculpturing was widely practised, artists turning out squat figures representing life on earth.

Towards the beginning of the twenty-first century B.C. civilisation in Sumer and Akkad began to decline again as a result of invasions by a less advanced people from Elam in the east. Then the domination of the Elamites was followed by that of the Semitic Amorites,[8] also a people of inferior civilisation who had infiltrated from the west. The Amorites founded, about 2050 B.C., the Babylonian Empire with its capital at Babylon. The sixth king in this state was Hammurabi (about 1750 B.C.), the greatest of Babylonian rulers. He brought all Mesopotamia under his sway and established the region's first really centralized government, complete with bureaucracy and military force. He amassed wealth through taxes and other collections from his subjects and devoted that wealth to the expansion of commerce, to land improvements, and to the establishment of Babylon. He also codified the laws, which constituted a definite advance in the establishment of control over human behaviour, and he encouraged the development of the arts and sciences.

The reign of Hammurabi was a high-water mark in Babylonian economic life. The period of prosperity was made possible by the maintenance of order, by drawing upon the natural resources of other areas, and by extending industrial production in royal, lordly, or temple households. Furthermore the high level of economic well-being was attained primarily by private enterprise, the Code of Hammurabi being very specific regarding the contractual rights of individuals and the status of private property.

A portion of the wealth that had been amassed by the time of Hammurabi was devoted to the arts and sciences. The Babylonians continued the astronomical observations of their predecessors and laid the foundations for a genuine science of mathematics upon which Hellenic and Arabic scholars were later to build modern mathematics. They developed place value, that is, a simplified form of numerical notation whereby the value of a sign is determined by its place in relation to other signs, like 1 *over* 3 and second decimal *place*; and by 1800 B.C. they had established certain geometrical relations, like Pythagoras's theorem. In their architecture, they continued the traditions of the Sumerians, although they endeavoured to relieve blank walls with sculpture, tiles, and carpets. In sculpture, their artists glorified the living and represented their gods in the form of man or mythical animals which have come down to us in heraldry and mythology—the gryphon, the dragon, the lion, and the bull. And in the field of literature, writers concentrated upon mythological and historical epics, some of which were incorporated in the Bible and hence are familiar to us, like the stories of the Creation, the Fall, and the Flood. In brief, the Babylonians developed those traditions of intellectual and artistic endeavour that had early become differentiated and fixed in Sumerian culture.

Soon after the reign of Hammurabi, which historians regard as the height of Babylonian civilisation, the political power and organisation of the Amorites was destroyed. Babylonia was torn by internal disorder and soon became the victim of foreign invaders. About 1650 B.C. the Kassites from the east of Babylon endeavoured to extend their dominion over the land, but throughout the 570 years of their rule they failed to create a strong central authority or to establish conditions conducive to economic strength and cultural achievement. Furthermore, long-range economic progress was curbed by the lack of technical innovations, the limited range of natural resources, the failure of a mass market to expand steadily, and a social attitude, which came from the institution of slavery, that was hostile to manual labour.

After a series of debilitating wars, Assyria to the north gained control of Babylon (729 B.C.), and Babylonia was not reconstituted as an independent state until 625 B.C. At the latter date consolidation of political power ushered in a new period of economic expansion, which led in the sixth century B.C. to a revival of civilising activity—to a kind of Neo-Babylonian renaissance. Subsequently Babylonia fell under Persian domination (538 B.C.), and then it was conquered by Alexander the Great (332 B.C.). Its heyday among the cultures of the world was then definitely past.

Other cultures of Hither Asia

Among the many peoples on the periphery of Babylonia, the most important were the Assyrians, Hittites, Mitanni, Persians, Syrians, Jews, and Phoenicians. Of them all we shall not treat in detail, for information about them is too scanty for purposes of our analysis, and some of them made no important contributions to transmissible knowledge which was to be handed down to Western culture. A word concerning the more prominent of these people will have to suffice.

One of the more important cultures of this group was the

Assyrian. It was located in the central Tigris region, where agriculture is restricted by a narrow plain and uncertain rainfall. Perhaps this fact accounts in part for the Assyrians' reliance upon war as a way of life. To be sure, they borrowed wholesale from the civilisation of the lower Mesopotamian region, taking over from the Sumerians, Akkadians, and Babylonians their techniques, their types of arms, their script, their learning, and to an extent their ideologies and art forms. Yet they remained peculiarly bellicose and ruthless and provide a classical example of a people who attempted to make war pay.[9]

That they had some success from such a policy is attested to by their large and imposing cities of Assur and Nineveh, their far-flung commercial outposts, and their ability to carry on extensive campaigns. Their prowess in arms was derived partly from their use of the horse and their ability to mobilize their resources but also partly from the development of certain military techniques—the heavily armed chariot, the battering-ram, and the assault tower. Their periods of greatest prosperity seem to be correlated with success in wars that gave them tribute or commercial advantages; and their periods of greatest economic decline coincide roughly with their reliance upon their own production or with failure in war.

During most of the second millennium B.C. the Assyrians withstood with only a moderate degree of success attacks from Egyptians, Hittites, Babylonians, and Mitanni. Towards the beginning of the eleventh century B.C., however, they were able to get control of the trade routes of Western Asia and to enjoy considerable prosperity. After a subsequent setback, Assur-nazir-pal II (883–859 B.C.) restored their position and obtained tribute from Phoenician cities. It was during his reign that Assyria experienced its classical period in architecture and art. After the conquest of Babylonia, which included the destruction of the city of Babylon (689 B.C.), and the conquest of Egypt (671 B.C.), Assyria enjoyed another period of economic and cultural success.

Then towards the end of the seventh century B.C., exhausted by extensive campaigns in Egypt and other far-distant places, the Assyrian Empire began to disintegrate and finally fell under the combined blows of Medes from Persia and Babylonians.

Of the Hittites, Mitanni, and Persians, we need say very little. The Hittites, located in central Asia Minor, created a feudal empire which through war and trade achieved its highest level of economic well-being in the thirteenth century B.C., which is the time in which the most important Hittite monuments were built. Then with migrations from the Aegean into their territory at the end of the second millennium B.C., their culture was swallowed up and disappeared as an independent entity. Similarly the Mitanni established an empire in the upper Tigris area, preyed upon their neighbours, enjoyed a brief period of economic success, and constructed their best buildings just prior to being brought to submission by Assyria (about 1275 B.C.). Finally the Persians, a people living in the Iranian plateau, developed a distinctive culture which attained its highest point of development in the sixth and fifth centuries B.C. It was in this period that Cyrus the Great (550–529 B.C.) founded an empire that extended from the Indus River to the Mediterranean and from the Caucasus to the Indian Ocean. The wealth drawn from this vast area permitted the construction of great palaces and a development of the arts. The Persian Empire threatened Greece in the fifth century B.C. but was finally demolished by Alexander the Great (336–330 B.C.). This conquest marked a definite decline in the civilisation of Persia.

In addition to these cultures of Hither Asia, we should mention briefly those along the coasts of Palestine, Phoenicia, Syria, and Cilicia. Here the land was for the most part mountainous and dry and did not provide important agricultural surpluses, as did Egypt and Mesopotamia. Nor were the people of these regions particularly warlike, so that they made little effort to live off others, as did the Assyrians and Hittites. Their chief economic advantage was that they were located along trade routes between centres of important cultures and could thus reap a profit from acting as middlemen. From the fourth millennium onward we find that they were engaging in commerce and carrying, that they exported what natural resources they had in excess of their own needs, notably timber and minerals, and that they borrowed industrial techniques from their neighbours for the production of such goods as textiles and pottery. Upon the basis of this economic activity they obtained a surplus which was able to maintain cities—Byblos, Tyre, Sidon, Tarsus, Aleppo, Damascus, and Jerusalem—and to achieve what by our definition was a moderately high degree of civilisation.

To determine with any degree of accuracy when peaks of economic well-being and of civilisation were reached in these cultures and what the correspondence between them was is extremely difficult. It is probably correct to say, however, that the Jews attained their greatest wealth following David's victories over the Philistines of the coast, that is, during the reign of Solomon (973–933 B.C.) and that the greatest cultural achievement of the Jews, the writing of the Old Testament, came mostly after this period. Phoenicia, for its part, probably reached the apex of its economic activity at about the beginning of the first millennium B.C., although by 1500 B.C. the people of the area had given a phonetic value to twenty-nine cuneiform characters taught them by the Babylonians and had thus established an alphabet.

Aegean culture

Beside the cultures of the Nile and of Hither Asia, the Bronze Age witnessed the development of another culture pertinent to our investigation—that of the Aegean Sea.[10] This region was bounded by Crete, Mycenae in the Peloponnesus, Troy at the western exit of the Hellespont, and the Syrian coast. Although the failure thus far to decipher the hieroglyphic tablets of this culture limits our knowledge of accomplishments, especially in science, literature, and law, archaeological remains give evidence of the attainment of a high degree of economic and cultural achievement. It was from this culture of the Aegean that Greek culture in its formative and most impressionable period borrowed many of its ideologies and patterns of behaviour.

The geographical environment of Aegean culture is markedly different from that of the river valleys that we have mentioned in connection with Egypt and Mesopotamia. The islands and coastlands of the Aegean have many arable sections, but they are so effectively divided by mountains and sea that the inhabitants were led, if not driven, to the sea. For its part, the sea is easily navigable, its many islands and mountainous shores providing landmarks for the navigator, and its numerous ports furnishing havens of retreat before the elements and for the loading and unloading of ships. In Aegean civilisations water transport on the sea played a role analogous to that of river transportation in Egypt and Mesopotamia.

Prior to about 3000 B.C. the Aegean region had two types of Neolithic culture with its improved stone tools and weapons, its domesticated animals, and its settled agriculture—that of the mainland and that of the island of Crete. By the early part of the third millennium B.C., however, a wave of invasions struck the Aegean and brought its various parts into contact one with the other. Some uninhabited places, like Cyprus, were settled; trade between Byblos and Egypt was increased; and techniques of copper metallurgy were introduced. Gradually the Aegean people moved out of the Neolithic Age into the Age of Copper, and as they did so the people of Crete acquired a position of primacy.

The island of Crete is relatively mountainous, and it is not rich in natural resources. The economic success that it achieved cannot, therefore, be attributed to an environment richly endowed by nature but rather to a strategic location, to easy access to markets, and to the enterprise of its people. Cretans turned early to manufacturing and to trade in manufactured goods. Soon after 3000 B.C. they were producing a distinctive pottery with bright colours on dark background which appealed to the tastes of the market; they were turning out metal products, particularly the triangular dagger, which were in great demand; and they were making commercially desirable stone and ivory carvings. Some of the raw materials for these products had to be imported, as, for example, copper from Cyprus (the Copper Island) and the Cyclades[11] and ivory from Egypt. These things the Cretans carried mostly in their own ships, for they had become excellent seamen, and they had a central position in the Eastern Mediterranean. In fact, they developed a thriving carrying trade and became the middlemen for the products of the entire Aegean. From this activity, they and the people of the Cyclades, who shared with them part of this development, accumulated a surplus above immediate needs which permitted the establishment of cities and the devotion of energies to cultural things.

About 2500 B.C. changes took place in the Aegean which further enhanced the situation of the Cretans. A new movement of population from Europe and Asia, associated with the Hittites coming into central Asia Minor, a new people into Thessaly, and the building of a second Troy on the ruins of the first, pushed the centre of Aegean culture southward towards Crete.

Then the introduction of bronze at about this time gave Crete another advantage, for the island was strategically located for receiving tin mined in Etruria, Spain, Gaul, Cornwall, and the Erz Mountains and for combining it with copper from Cyprus. Finally the proximity of Crete to Egypt made it possible to benefit from trade with that highly developed area. The superiority that Crete achieved in bronze, as, for example, in the long bronze dagger, was soon extended to other trades—to pottery turned on the wheel, finished as faïence, and decorated with polychrome, to gold-working, and to engraving. Reliance upon imported raw materials and exported processed goods made necessary the development of a great merchant marine and a mastery of the sea.

For about a millennium, from 2500 to 1400 B.C., the great sea power, or thalassocracy, which was Crete maintained its economic, cultural, and maritime hegemony in the Aegean. Large palaces were built in cities like Knossos, which were a combination of apartments, workshops, storehouses, and sanctuaries. These palaces were adorned with colonnades and frescoes of profusion and beauty. From the necessity of keeping records of business activity in these beehives, Cretan writing is believed to have come. It passed from the ideographic to the hieroglyphic script stage about 2000 B.C. and was further simplified in the succeeding quarter millennium. Of the political life of the island we know little, although it is thought that unity was achieved and some federation or working arrangement existed between the Cretans and their neighbours. In about 1750 B.C. some misfortune befell the island, probably a revolution or civil war, which resulted in the destruction of the great palaces in the leading cities. Within a short time, however, new palaces, more beautiful and more richly decorated than the first, were constructed, and Cretan industry and art were flourishing once again. Buildings, pottery, jewellery, swords, and frescoes testify to beauty of design and exquisite workmanship. In fact, during the sixteenth and fifteenth centuries B.C. Crete achieved the acme of its artistic production—its classical period.

All was not well, however, in the Cretan scene. During and following the troubles in Egypt attendant upon the domination of the Hyksos (1680–1580 B.C.), the Cretans intensified their activity in the Aegean Sea region itself. In the process of exporting its goods, Crete exported also its institutions, methods of organization, its techniques, its styles, and some of its people. Thus Cretan civilisation was literally expanding overseas. In some places this development could be controlled by Crete to its own advantage, but in others the maintenance of a dominant position was impossible. This was particularly true in Mycenae and Tiryns in Argolis. Here the barbarian Achaeans, who had come from the Danube Valley about 3000 B.C. and had subsequently occupied all Hellas, seemed particularly adept at borrowing from Crete and at the same time in maintaining their own independence. Perhaps these towns had certain locational advantages in being able to draw on more resources, to control a larger market, or to obtain cheaper labour. Whatever the reasons, they began the manufacture of "Cretan goods" which they transported in their own ships and protected with their own navy. Their more standardized products appear to have had an advantage over those of Crete, which were becoming more flowery and were destined more exclusively for the luxury trade.

About 1400 B.C. a devastating blow hit Crete. Its cities, no longer fortified because of a consummate confidence in the protection of the sea and in a naval arm, were laid waste. Cretan supremacy was at an end. Whether the destruction of Crete was effected by invading Mycenaeans or whether it was wrought by internal revolution is not certain. Yet the fact remains that for the next two centuries Mycenae was to dominate the Aegean world. Production in Crete deteriorated, as is witnessed by the substitution of clay for stone and metal vessels and the paucity of archaeological finds of Cretan goods in other areas. On the other hand, production in the Hellas of the Achaeans increased considerably. Its cities grew rapidly; its wares were distributed throughout the Aegean; and its supply of hard-to-get raw materials, like tin, seems to have been abundant. Although art forms, workmanship, and a decline in writing all testify to retrogression in the intellectual and cultural aspects of Aegean life, a concentration upon the production of staples and the export of these staples brought wealth to Hellas—to the Hellas described with poetic licence in the *Iliad* as being as opulent as Egypt.

Along with this economic development the Achaeans of Mycenae and other important cities embarked upon a policy of

THE CULTURE OF THE AEGEAN

expansion—either by peaceful penetration, outright conquest, or a combination of the two. Gradually all the Aegean came under their influence. But the Achaeans over-reached themselves, as have so many peoples in the past. Although they were successful against the small states which could not draw upon the organized resources of a large area and even against Troy and its allies in the war celebrated in the *Iliad* and *Odyssey*, they were crushed in their efforts to invade Egypt (about 1229 B.C.). This defeat marked the end of Achaean expansion and together with other expeditions sapped some of the strength of Hellas itself. Gradually bands of barbarians from Albania, the Dorians, closely related to the Achaeans in language, pushed southward. By 1200 B.C. what had begun as infiltration became invasion. Rapidly the newcomers over-ran Hellas, pushing the Achaeans before them on to the coasts of Asia Minor and on to Aegean islands, while the inhabitants of these places in turn attacked both Hittites and Egyptians. This was part of the movement of the "People of the Sea." In their wake the Dorians left little but destruction of the Aegean bronze culture, yet out of this destruction was to arise a new and more glorious civilisation—that of the Greeks.

As one reflects on this rapid survey of ancient-empire cultures, certain generalizations take shape which are worth careful consideration. When techniques of production became stabilized, efforts to increase output of goods and services consisted primarily (1) in the exploitation of new resources either by land reclamation, commerce, or conquest and (2) in a more efficient organization of production and of distribution by a deepening of investment, a division of labour, the use of money, and better transportation. The success of these efforts depended to a large extent upon political unification of large areas to provide peace at home and victory abroad. In the process of unification, however, rulers frequently attained so much power that they effected a concentration of wealth which, on the one hand, permitted them to support the arts but, on the other, militated against the general sharing of the benefits of civilisation and aroused the hostility of subordinate lords.

During the Bronze Age peaks of production appear to have been concomitants of peace or of successful foreign war and to have had a close relationship to the most generally recognized peaks of civilising achievement. Furthermore, concepts of what a civilisation should strive for—whether material gain, a future life, scientific achievement, artistic expression, or dominion over others—took shape at an early date. Similarly the forms that much of this activity was to follow were established towards the beginning of a culture's history and changed, if at all, only after some devastating experience. In the formation of standards and forms all the factors of human existence—economic, social, political, intellectual, and religious—came into play.

One aspect of the process, however, stood out as particularly arresting, that is, the manner in which one culture borrowed from another and built upon the borrowed product. Geographic proximity of one culture to another, degree of intercourse and dependence between them, the adaptability and usefulness of the borrowed part in the environment of the borrower, and some degree of similarity between what was borrowed and the technique or institution that it replaced seem to have been the controlling forces in determining what was acquired. Finally the highest degrees of civilisation, as we have defined the word, appear to have been achieved not by cultures that placed emphasis upon war but by the more peace-loving and industrious peoples.

Footnotes to Chapter III

1 This was effected by heating sand and natron (sodium carbonate), which was found in its natural state. The process of making clear glass was essentially similar to that of making a glaze for pottery (faïence). Glass was at first cast or moulded. It was not blown until the Roman Period.

2 Dates prior to 2000 B.C. are difficult to determine with accuracy. Consequently chronologies employed by various scholars differ for these early periods. The author has endeavoured to use those dates most generally accepted and those that indicate the correct relations of time in the civilisations treated. The date for the Code of Hammurabi, crucial to early chronology, has recently been changed from about 1950 B.C. to about 1750 B.C.

3 Some scholars are of the opinion that the cultural developments of the Sixth Dynasty (2420–2270 B.C.) were greater than those of the Third.

4 There had been improvement in the political situation under the Eleventh Dynasty (2100–2000 B.C.), but the reign ended in war and famine.

5 Crete may also have paid tribute for a short period.

6 This was the religious reform of Amenhotep IV, who took the name of Ikhnaton (1375–1358 B.C.).

7 The Bible story of the building of the Tower of Babel stemmed without doubt from the construction of a ziggurat.

8 Semitic refers to a linguistic and not a racial group.

9 An example of their ruthlessness was their forceful displacement of entire populations in an effort to consolidate their power.

10 This civilisation is sometimes referred to as Minoan after Minos, legendary king of Knossos in Crete. It is also called Cretan. Both of these names seem too restrictive. The term "Aegean" accords best with the facts in the case.

11 The islands extending south-eastward from Attica.

For Further Reading

James Baikie, *A History of Egypt from the Earliest Times to the End of the XVIII Dynasty* (1939), 2 Vols.

J. H. Breasted, *A History of the Ancient Egyptians* (1920)

Louis Delaporte, *Mesopotamia: The Babylonian and Assyrian Civilisations* (1925)

F. M. Feldhaus, *Technik der Antike und des Mittelalters* (1931)

Gustave Glotz, *The Aegean Civilisation* (1925)

A. T. Olmstead, *History of Assyria* (1923)

——— *A History of Palestine and Syria to the Macedonian Conquest* (1931)

J. D. S. Pendlebury, *The Archaeology of Crete: an Introduction* (1939)

Jacques Pirenne, *Les Grands courants de l'histoire* (1945 *ff.*)

A. P. Usher, *A History of Mechanical Inventions* (1929)

Quincy Wright, *A Study of War* (1944), 2 Vols.

IV

ANCIENT GREECE

Dᴜʀɪɴɢ the thousand years prior to the birth of Christ, there was a shift in the location of the most advanced cultures from Hither Asia and Egypt, north-westward to the European continent, first to Greece and then to Rome. These cultures, borrowing heavily from their predecessors, attained higher levels of civilisation than had ever been reached before. Greek culture was particularly brilliant; and from it Western culture was eventually to draw many of its concepts, art styles, bodies of knowledge, and ideologies. So great is our heritage from Greece that in retrospect the shift in centres of civilisation from Asia to Europe constitutes for us one of the most important facts of history.

Reasons for Greek primacy—a general statement

That people in the Grecian peninsula should have amassed enough economic surplus to permit the establishment of a high level of civilisation is astonishing in view of the small size of their territory and the innate poverty of their land. Greece comprises an area comparable to that of the State of New York, but only 20 per cent. of its surface can be cultivated because of mountains. Furthermore, it lacks mineral resources for industrial production or navigable rivers for internal transportation. What it does have are numerous ports, easy access to navigable seas, and a location that favours communication with neighbouring lands.

In spite of the limited amount of arable land, the Greeks

produced specialized agricultural goods which became articles of trade in commerce with other regions. They also began the manufacture of industrial products for export and performed certain services, like shipping and banking, for foreign peoples. In return for what they sold abroad, Greeks received foodstuffs and raw materials. To a large extent the skill of Greek workmen the ability of Greek enterprisers to organize production, the acumen of Greek traders, and the aptitude of Greek protagonists to establish a foreign demand for Greek goods made possible the obtaining of what could not be produced in sufficient supply within Greece itself.

Between the sixth and third centuries B.C. Greece was in varying degrees the "workshop of the ancient world." As is usually the case when the products of skill and enterprise are exchanged for raw materials and foodstuffs, the producers of primary products devoted more hours of labour to each unit of value than did the producers of finished goods and services. Hence the Greeks reaped an important economic benefit from the exchange. In many respects, therefore, the economic position of Greece was analogous to that of Crete in the heyday of its primacy in Aegean culture or to that of Great Britain in the nineteenth century. As in these instances, the continued welfare of Greece depended upon the supplying of goods and services to foreign markets, upon mastery of the sea, and upon the fact that her customers did not produce those things that could be obtained from Greece. Ultimately Greece failed to maintain these conditions, for other peoples acquired Greek techniques of production and of trade and could match her in the arts of war. They became economically independent of Greece and with their superior resources and power were able by force to strike down a divided country. When this happened, Greek civilisation relative to that of other countries declined.

As in the other cultures that we have treated, so also in Greece the accumulation of economic surplus was followed by a high level of civilisation. In the case of the empire cultures of Hither Asia, however, surplus for cultural activity was located primarily in the hands of a small number of rulers, their officials, and priests. In Greece, on the other hand, surplus was acquired by landholders, manufacturers, traders, bankers, and shippers, who, although they effected a considerable concentration of wealth, constituted a fairly large number of persons. Because these people were free to use their wealth as they saw fit, a situation developed in which a comparatively larger segment of society than we have encountered hitherto was able to exercise its creative talents. Indeed many of the artistic and intellectual giants of Greece were the sons of well-to-do businessmen.

Wealth and its relatively wide distribution in ancient Greece were basic factors in the development of civilisation in Greece, but there were also many more specific reasons for its accomplishment. One of these was the fact that Greeks came into contact with peoples of many different cultures and borrowed heavily from them. Thus they acquired a large body of knowledge, techniques, and standards of accomplishment from which they could proceed to greater heights. Furthermore, their economy was of a kind that led to the concentration of activity in urban centres, and, as we have seen, urban environment seems to have been best for civilising accomplishment. In cities intellectuals and artists could congregate, exchange ideas, and find competitive inspiration. Then, too, the Greek lack of political centralization and the absence of a common religion, well-established priesthood, and a sacred book contributed to keeping the mind unfettered by dogma. The secular attitude of the Greeks helped to develop an inquisitiveness and a curiosity which led them to ask all manner of questions about nature, politics, philosophy, and art. They challenged traditional beliefs and permitted a considerable amount of individual lee-way regarding them. In fact, Greek inquisitiveness seems to have gone hand-in-hand with a large degree of intellectual tolerance.

In the absence of an over-weening religion, the Greeks were free to turn their attention to the most amazing thing that their sensory organs could encompass—to nature. Not only did they come to admire nature, but they attempted to idealize it in art, to understand it in their science, and to control it by their technology.

Apt as these generalizations about ancient Greece are, the reader should realize that they are based on the cumulative and culminating experience of the Greeks. They began to be apparent in the formative period of Greek culture from the twelfth to the sixth century B.C. They were clearly applicable to the period of greatest economic and cultural success from the sixth to the middle of the fourth century B.C. They become less sharply delineated in the period of the diffusion of Greek culture (the Hellenistic Period) from the end of the fourth to the first century B.C. They are introduced here merely to serve as guideposts for what is to follow.

The formative period of Greek culture, 1100 to 600 B.C.

The formative period of Greek culture was inaugurated by widespread changes, which resulted from mass migrations that in turn were probably caused by rapid increases in population, by drought, or by both. In any case, near the close of the second millennium B.C., as we have previously remarked, peoples in the food-gathering stage of economic development or people at least with only a partially settled agriculture pushed into districts that had a completely settled agriculture and a degree of urban life.

These migrations of the so-called "Peoples of the Sea" were amazingly far-flung, occurring all the way from the Danube Valley to the plains of China. In the Middle East the Medes and Persians, who had probably come from the Caucasus, moved into Iran and there developed, as we have seen, a power that was to be a threat to Greece. Somewhat earlier out of the Arabian desert had come the Aramaeans, the Habiru, or Hebrews, and the Phoenicians, but now the Aramaeans invaded Babylonia, the Hebrews moved northward into Palestine, and the Phoenicians began to establish trading posts in the Western Mediterranean and to gobble up sea trade. Into Greece came Dorians, who pushed many of the occupying Achaeans out. This pressure led to the attack of the Achaeans on Egypt, 1198 to 1167 B.C., to the Achaean Wars with Troy,[1] which are the subject of the Homeric poems, and to the settlement of the Achaeans upon the coasts of Asia Minor. Thus at the end of the second millennium B.C. Greece was partly settled by newcomers, and many of the previous inhabitants were squeezed in among various peoples on the eastern shore of the Aegean Sea.[2] In these two groups Greek culture was to take form.

Civilisation seems to have suffered as a result of the coming of these people of less advanced culture into regions occupied by people of more highly developed cultures. Archaeological evidence bears ample testimony to a decline in production in the last two centuries of the second millennium B.C., to a crudeness of craftsmanship, and to a reduction in trade. Yet this period was by no means a total cultural black-out. Assyria, which had suffered the least, was still collecting Sumerian, Akkadian, and Babylonian texts for its libraries. Astronomical studies continued to be made in both Assyrian and Babylonian temple observatories. Business practices were kept alive by peoples like the Phoenicians. Much craft lore was preserved, if not advanced, by workers throughout the civilised world. Nor among Greeks either on the mainland or along the coasts of Anatolia did the invasions result in a complete reversion to Neolithic standards. Pottery continued to be made on the wheel and to be decorated in the late Mycenaean manner. The Aegean arts of seamanship were never entirely wiped out. And cheap iron weapons and tools were being made to replace more costly bronze products.

So, although the beginnings of the Iron Age were accompanied by a dark age—darker perhaps and certainly more general than that which had ushered in the Bronze Age—retrogression was not complete. Recovery from the effects of invasion required, however, the expenditure of an enormous amount of energy and nearly half a millennium of time. The Greeks who led the general revival were those who had settled on the coasts of Anatolia. As late as the sixth century B.C. the most active economic and cultural life of Hellas was to be found there, and not until the fifth century B.C. was the supremacy of mainland Greeks clearly established. Thus, although the greatest heights of Greek culture were attained on the European mainland, we must give consideration to Greeks on both sides of the Aegean.

One of Greece's most characteristic institutions, the city-state, appeared in the formative period among both the Ionian Greeks on the eastern shores of the Aegean and the Dorian Greeks of the mainland. The former found themselves crowded into small enclaves with the sea on one side, hostile natives on the other, and mountains between their settlements. The logic of their geographic situation dictated strong, local political regimes in which they would be the masters and natives (foreigners to them) would be without political rights. In mainland Greece, the topography of which is characterized by juxtaposed, cup-shaped valleys, the rims of the cups being lofty mountains, there was similarly an early tendency towards localism. There the aristocracy of the invaders took possession of the better lands in the valleys, created strongholds to protect their holdings, and established political regimes which limited rights of citizenship. So on both sides of the Aegean the city-state became a fixture— and such a firm one that political unification of the entire Greek people proved to be impossible. This fact is of utmost importance in understanding Greek history. It meant that with many independent rulers the assumption of divine rights by any one individual, as in the Eastern monarchies, was made extremely difficult. It meant, too, that the Greeks were seldom, if ever, able to concentrate all their strength in aggressive foreign policy or in defence and that they were badgered eternally by inter-city wars which sapped their energies and ultimately invited foreign invasion.

As the institution of the Greek city-state began to take shape, so, too, the economy of Greece started to assume its characteristic form. At the beginning of the first millennium B.C. Greek economic activity was largely agricultural with concentration on the growing of grains and livestock for subsistence.[3] Gradually, however, commerce and industry began to appear, particularly among Ionian Greeks. Situated as they were on the coast of Asia Minor and hemmed in by hostile natives, they found it impossible to expand their holdings of land to take care of a growing population. In their predicament they began to specialize on the vine and the olive in order to get goods that could be used in exchange for grain. Subsequently they started the making of industrial articles in order further to supplement their food supply through commerce. And as they did so they acquired from their neighbours much of the technological heritage of Egypt and of Mesopotamia.

With the production of wine, olive oil, and industrial goods beyond their own needs, the Greeks of Anatolia engaged in a search for markets for their goods and for sources of supply for the things that they wanted. Ultimately they obtained fish and grain from Italy and Sicily, the Balkan peninsula, the Straits, and the Black Sea; they imported silver, gold, copper, and iron from a score of places; and they got large quantities of leather and wool from their neighbours in the interior of Asia Minor. They developed commercial fleets, regularized trade, and got control of most of Aegean carrying and commerce. Then, as the scope of their economic life became broader, many of them migrated to places with which they did business. In this way they spread their techniques and also aspects of their culture over a wide area.

Among the regions influenced directly by this development

was mainland Greece itself. There large landowners began to give up grain culture for the more profitable vine and olive, thus adding two important goods to livestock as articles of trade. The production of wine and oil encouraged slavery, for vines and olive trees could be tended successfully by slave labour, and slavery contributed to the commercial character of the economy. Furthermore, industry was expanded, particularly pottery, textile manufacture, iron and other metal-working, and ship building. Concomitantly the mainland Greeks started to do their own carrying and trading and to make themselves independent of the Phoenicians, the traditional "peddlers of the sea."

Then in the eighth and seventh centuries B.C. a mass migration from Greece took place, a movement that was analogous to, but on a larger scale than, the expansion overseas of Ionian Greeks. The reasons for this exodus are extremely complex. Apparently overcrowding in the cities led to the establishment of colonies to which the urban poor flocked. It is also probable that slave labour in agriculture so worsened the conditions of poor farmers that they sought relief by going abroad. And then there were some migrants, as is always the case, who left the homeland in search of great riches or to satisfy their curiosity and love of adventure. But whatever the impelling forces may have been, the expansion was remarkable in its extent. Settlements were made in Sicily, in southern Italy, which came to be known as Magna Graecia, or Great Greece, in Gaul, in Spain, in the Straits, in the Black Sea region, in Cyprus, in Egypt, and in Libya.

The expansion of Greece was also important for its effects on the homeland. Now the resources of a much larger area than hitherto could be drawn upon for the benefit of Greeks—and this fact made possible the success of Greek industrial and commercial activity in the sixth to the fourth centuries B.C. Also, Greece acquired new techniques from the cultures with which she came in contact. Finally, close association with people of other cultures stimulated that inquisitive attitude of the Greek mind which dominated Greek intellectual life in the succeeding four centuries.

The formative period of Greek culture was marked, then, in its economic aspects by a great development of industry and commerce, by the expansion of Greece overseas, and by the consequent amassing of considerable economic surplus. In time accumulated wealth permitted Greeks to devote part of their energies to the extension of knowledge and to the production of works of art. In the creation of these intellectual and aesthetic aspects of life, Greece was a heavy borrower. From Aegean culture it inherited techniques of bronze metallurgy, methods of making pottery, and artistic standards of a high order. Similarly, from late Mycenaean architecture Greece borrowed the basic pattern for its most noteworthy architectural structures—the temples—a pattern that persisted without fundamental alteration throughout Greek history. And from Mycenaean and Eastern sources Ionian Greeks adopted their earliest styles of painting and sculpture—adoptions that were less stiff and formal than the originals.

Greeks were, however, originators as well as borrowers, and their creative talents were clearly marked during the first five centuries of their history. For example, Greek religion did not follow the arbitrary absolutes of Eastern creeds but tended to glorify man. Thus local Greek deities, like Athena at Athens, were worshipped as symbols of glory and power of the city-states, while national gods, like Apollo, were revered for the degree to which they possessed human virtues. In fact, the discovery of man, that is, interest in all phases of man's life, was perhaps the Greeks' greatest achievement.[4] This glorification of man resulted in an extension of the individual's intellectual freedom and an increase in the range of opportunities for alternative decisions in intellectual and aesthetic matters.

The Greeks were also originators in their extension of control over human environment. With the creation of the city-state a step was taken towards weakening arbitrary, tribal monarchy, towards government by the corporate action of citizens, and towards rule according to man-made law. In establishing control over physical environment, Greeks displayed creative ability, particularly in securing foodstuffs and raw materials from abroad through the development of trade. And although they were not renowned for technological innovations, they did improve agricultural methods, advance mining techniques, and develop iron metallurgy.

Perhaps the greatest genius of the Greeks was, however, in the realm of the intellect and in aesthetics. Indeed some of the most remarkable achievements of all time in these two areas are of Greek origin. In the formative period of Greek culture this particular propensity may be illustrated by the *Iliad* and *Odyssey*, poems sung by court minstrels in Ionia and possibly brought together by an actual Homer in the ninth century B.C. These epics are a glorification of Greek history; they show pride in workmanship and a search for technical perfection; they establish as virtues honour, courage, and discipline, and patriotism; and they glorify man and his power in winning the favour of the gods. Here were standards and views which were set early in Greek history and which influenced Greek life for more than half a millennium.

Greek culture from the sixth to the fourth century B.C.

With the expansion of Greece overseas, the formative period of Greek culture and of Greek economy came to an end. It was succeeded from the sixth to the fourth century by the most illustrious period of Greek history. In these two centuries Greece attained her maximum wealth and achieved her highest degree of civilisation.

As has already been intimated, economic well-being in the second period of Greek history was largely dependent upon commerce with overseas areas; and commerce, in its turn, relied

Black Sea

THRACE

Byzantium

MYSIA

Sardis

Smyrna

IONIA

Ephesus

LYDIA

Halicarnassus

THASOS

LESBOS

Mytilene

Chios

SAMOS

Miletus

RHODES

MACEDONIA

Amphipolis

THESSALY

Mt Olympus

Aegean Sea

Chalcis

Marathon

Euboea

DELOS

CRETE

EPIRUS

ATTICA

Athens

Aegina

MELOS

Corcyra

PELOPONNESUS

Argos

Thermopylae
Delphi
Megara
Corinth
Sparta

Tarentum

MAGNA GRAECIA

Sybaris

Croton

Ionian Sea

Locri

Elea

Messana

Rhegium

Naxos

Cumae

SICILY

Syracuse

Agrigentum

Thalassa

MILES
0   50   100   200

THE CULTURE OF GREECE

heavily upon shipping. Here the Greeks were particularly success-ful. They adopted the trireme, a ship with three banks of rowers. Invented as early as the eighth century, this vessel was able to make headway when winds were contrary and to carry as much as 250 tons' burden. As the size of the ship was thus increased, the Greeks improved their ports with breakwaters and docks. They also developed their seamanship, navigators greatly extend-ing their knowledge of Mediterranean geography, weather, and winds.

Gradually the Greeks encroached on the carrying of the Phoenicians, whose sphere of dominance became restricted primarily to the North African coast west of Carthage. Greek ships henceforth found their way to Naucratis in Egypt, the Syrian ports, to the Black Sea, the Italian peninsula, to Marseilles, to Spain, and probably to the Isle of Wight. To these places Greek merchantmen carried textiles, pottery, iron weapons and tools, works of art, jewellery, and leather goods and brought back grains, dried fruits, salt fish, metals, hides, amber, ivory, wool, and timber.

Many Greek ports were involved in this trade, and as time went on sea routes tended to converge at centres that enjoyed particular locational advantages—at such places as Miletus on the Anatolian coast and as Delos in the Aegean Islands. By the fifth century B.C. Piraeus, the port of Athens, was probably the most prominent focal point for shipping in mainland Greece, and the ports of Corinth, on either side of the isthmus that forms the extreme wasp waist of Greece, were close rivals in importance. Here ships frequently broke cargo to avoid the stormy voyage round the coasts of the Peloponnesus or to trade in nearby markets. That the ports of Athens and Corinth ranked so high among Greek shipping centres is important to remember, for the great cultural achievements of Greece were realized in places like these rather than in the less commercial and more agricultural cities like Sparta.

Overseas trade had a direct bearing upon the development of Greek business institutions, especially upon the increased use of money, credit, and banking services. The first coins, pieces of metal whose quality and weight were guaranteed by a state, appeared in Lydia, a neighbour of the Anatolian Greeks, about 700 B.C. Not long afterwards coins of large denomination began to be issued by Greek city-states, and shortly after 600 B.C. coins of small denomination were minted. As has been previously stated, money oils the wheels of commerce. Thus it was in Greece. Small coins had, moreover, a new and almost revolutionary effect. With the extension of a money economy to the lowest classes, the small landowner or the small artisan could produce his goods for a wider market, and he could more readily store up surplus, either for the extension of his enterprise or for the purchase of objects of refinement—from jewellery to education.

With the increased use of money there was also a development of banking. The great variety of coins that came into existence called for a group of specialists in exchange—the money-changers —and soon these men were drawing up contracts for their clients, receiving money for safe keeping, and making loans. In essence what these bankers did was to accumulate wealth from many persons, even from those of small means, and to make it available to enterprising persons, presumably for increasing the output of goods or for augmenting the supply of services. To facilitate the transfer of money, Greek bankers developed the letter of credit, the bill of exchange, and the book-keeping clearing of accounts among individuals. Bankers also made bottomry loans, whereby a skipper would borrow on his cargo but would be relieved of his responsibility to pay his debt if the cargo did not arrive at its destination. This was one of the first attempts at a dispersion of risks for a premium—an elementary form of insurance.

Finally, the use of money gave rise to a price system—to a relationship of market value between goods and whatever metals were used in coins, whether it was gold, silver, or copper. The price system in itself was extremely important, for as gold, silver, or copper coins commanded more or fewer goods, the burden of paying debts, of collecting from one's creditors, and of remunerating labour (wages usually lag behind prices) fluctuated accordingly. In Athens, where most of these developments were carried farthest and where the famous Laureion silver mines produced a supply of silver, prices for grains, olive oil, and livestock rose by over 500 per cent. from the end of the sixth century to the end of the fourth. To some of the effects of this price rise we shall refer later.

In spite of the fact that the state played a role in the development of the Greek monetary system, Greek economic progress was achieved under what was fundamentally a system of *laissez faire*. Especially in foreign commerce a policy of free trade was pursued, for Greek exports competed favourably for a long time with goods of foreign origin. Besides, customs barriers would have endangered the system of exchange by which Greece exported goods in order to get absolutely essential imports. What state intervention in economic affairs did exist was of a character to facilitate trade and not to impair it, like enforcement of the laws of contract, the establishment of standard weights and measures, and the building of roads and harbours. Moreover, the Greeks permitted anyone, including foreigners and slaves, to engage in commerce and often granted citizenship to the wealthiest of such groups.

Important as trade was to the economic life of Greece, industry was its ever-present companion. Without industrial production the Greeks would have had little to exchange for the foodstuffs and raw materials which they needed, and accordingly they could not have supported as large a population as they did. Indeed the production and exportation of goods are a substitute for emigration. When production and exportation were being conducted satisfactorily, Greece sustained a large population that contended successfully with powers like Persia, which embraced vastly more territory than she. When they were not being managed well, Greek migration took place.

The success of Greek industry has been the object of much speculation, for a simple explanation is not apparent. The peninsula had no particular advantages in natural resources, as we have seen, although it did have some outcroppings of iron ore, some copper, lead, and silver from the Laureion mines near Athens, and timber for building and industry. Nor did its people introduce revolutionary techniques, although they displayed a certain inventiveness by the development of the ship with three banks of rowers and by the improvement of siege weapons. The Greeks did not employ any great amount of power from inanimate sources, although they knew about the expansive properties of steam, at least in the Hellenistic Period, the force of falling water, and the transmission of power by mechanical means. Furthermore, the demands of the market were never so great, sudden, or persistent that they could not be met by speeding up, or by adding to, the existing system of production.

Greek industrial success seems to have been based largely upon an ability to achieve low production and distribution costs. And this advantage was derived from a division of labour and from providing workers with superior equipment, particularly tools. The specialization of industrial tasks had reached a point by the end of the fifth century where, for example, in the woollen industry, there were workers who devoted themselves primarily to the following tasks: shearing, washing wool, carding, spinning, weaving, fulling, and dyeing. In most trades specialized tasks were performed in small shops, but in a few rare instances producing establishments were large, one *entrepreneur* at the Laureion mines employing a thousand slaves. As time went on, workers acquired better equipment, for tools made from iron were superior to those of bronze. Indeed a reasonable proportion of earnings went into investments for producer goods—for goods with which to make more goods.[5]

Greek industrial success was also dependent upon the labour supply. In general, workers were divided into four main categories —freeborn citizens, freeborn foreigners or *metics*, freed slaves, and slaves. Slaves, obtained as a result of debt, war, or purchase, comprised an estimated one-third of the 300,000 persons living in Athens at the close of the fifth century. Whether or not they provided labour at low cost is disputed, but they certainly furnished a steady and fairly abundant source of labour. Free men were paid in fifth-century Athens enough to provide them with some margin beyond their basic expenditures, but their wages failed to rise as fast as prices with the result that between the sixth and fourth centuries B.C. their real wages, that is, the amount of goods and services that they could actually obtain with their wages, declined, perhaps by one-half.

Such a situation usually acts in the short run as a stimulant to production, if there is an adequate market for goods, because employers find that labour costs are relatively low and profits are high. For a time this relationship of wages to profits—or profit inflation, as it has been called—reacted favourably upon Greek industry. But in time a lag of wages behind prices may have other consequences—it may lead to civil strife and to a limitation of the market because of the low purchasing power of workers. There is evidence to show that Greece experienced this result in the second half of the fourth century B.C.

In addition to those factors in Greek industrial development already mentioned, four others were certainly of importance. In many times and places throughout history societies have developed a contempt for participation in industrial and commercial enterprise. Although such an attitude prevailed in Greek cities like Sparta and Thebes, where the economy was largely agricultural and where government was in the hands of a rich agricultural aristocracy, it was by no means general. In industrial and commercial cities, like Athens and Corinth, business was not regarded as civilly degrading, and for the most part not as degrading at all.

Second, the policies of city-states frequently had an important bearing upon industrial development. At Athens, Themistocles's policy in the first part of the fifth century of devoting the state's profit from the mines of Laureion to the building of a fleet and a port gave industry and trade an enormous boost. Similarly, Pericles's policy of rebuilding the city after the Persian Wars gave a stimulus to economic activity.

Third, Greek industry and commerce were conducted, at least in the fifth century B.C., largely for profit in a wide and impersonal market rather than for the satisfaction of known needs in a local market. Here was the germ, at least, of the capitalist system which on a much greater scale was to characterize the economy of Western culture. Fourth, the question arises of the extent of capital formation and investment during the sixth, fifth, and first part of the fourth centuries B.C. In the industrial and commercial cities capital accumulation was apparently extensive. For the most part the ancient Greeks do not seem to have indulged in extravagant personal expenditure but rather to have encouraged thrift and savings. At all events, we know of individual cases of large fortunes being used in productive enterprise.

Before concluding this section on Greek economic development in its most prosperous period, something should be said about agriculture. In spite of the fact that industry and commerce were responsible for the larger portion of the economic surplus available in Greece, the majority of the Greeks found employment on the land. We have already mentioned the cultivation of the vine and the olive, to which might be added the fig, as commercial crops. Their development encroached upon the use of land for the growing of grain in which Greece became deficient. Yet total agricultural production probably increased during the period under review even though it did not meet the requirements of the expanding population. New land was brought into cultivation by irrigation, drainage, and forest clearance.[6] A greater abundance of iron tools served also to increase the productivity of Greek farmers. Then the Greeks learned by experience some of the uses of fertilizers. They realized the benefit of humus to the soil and spread the manure of their livestock on the land; and in addition they used chemical fertilizers—wood ashes (potash), nitrates, and lime. And they even practised the rotation of crops to avoid leaving part of their land to lie fallow.

With the commercialization of agriculture there was a tendency towards the concentration of holdings in large estates. Perhaps the chief impelling element in this trend was the need for relatively large amounts of capital to finance the bringing into production of the vine, the olive, and the fig tree and for acquiring slaves to do the work. In any case, in states like Sparta where agriculture retained its position of primacy in economic activity, land became concentrated in the hands of a few—from 9,000 owners in the early sixth century to about a hundred in the middle of the second century B.C. Even in the more democratic states, large land-holdings were not uncommon, although in some places, notably Athens, public policy favoured the preservation of the "family" farm.

Thus it came about that through agricultural activity on a large scale, as well as from commerce and industry, economic surplus was amassed which allowed the Greeks to devote a larger part of their energies to intellectual and aesthetic matters. It was clearly in this middle period of Greek history from 600 to 400 B.C. that the greatest proportion of Greek wealth was so employed and that Greek civilisation attained its acme. Then, for example, Greek cities had their greatest growth and built their most famous buildings.[7] Consequently, architects had great opportunities to put their talents to work,[8] and in doing so developed rules of proportion which account in large part for the beauty of Greek structures. They evolved excellent dimensions for their columns, worked out new styles of columns, the simpler Doric type giving way to the more ornate Ionic and Corinthian, and they found a happy solution to the place of sculpture in architecture. So far as sculpture and painting were concerned, Greek artists freed themselves from earlier rigidities and Oriental influences and made every effort to render human form in a more naturalistic manner, to glorify nature in every way. In both of these arts there appeared to be a fuller knowledge of anatomy,[9] a technical ability to portray likenesses,[10] and fine craftsmanship, which is an indicator of high aesthetic accomplishment.[11] In painting, important advances were made towards an understanding, although never a complete one, of perspective.

In letters this period saw the epic poet give way to the lyric poet,[12] the creation of the tragedy and the comedy,[13] and the appearance of historical prose. The tragedy was one of the most distinctive and most brilliant achievements of the Greeks. It portrayed the play of human emotions over human problems and through excellence of craftsmanship and concentration on a single theme attained a power seldom equalled in literary expression. Historical literature, the first literary prose of the Greeks, showed a desire to know other peoples,[14] to understand the forces at work in society,[15] and to present the past in an agreeable manner.[16]

In this same middle period of Greek history that inquisitiveness of mind to which we have already referred found expression in philosophy—in speculation concerning the origins of the universe, the facts and laws of nature, and the principles of human conduct. The first evidence of such speculation was found in Ionian cities in the sixth century B.C. and took such form as the atomic theory—that the universe was made by atoms floating in space which from inward necessity formed the universe as it is. From these Ionian beginnings two currents of thought are distinguishable, the one concerned with the collection and organization of observable data and the other with deductive reasoning about how we know things and what we know.

In the former current was Thales of Miletus, who forecast correctly an eclipse of the sun in 585 B.C. and who introduced geometry from Egypt. Here also should be placed Pythagoras (582–507 B.C.) who advanced the system of theorems and proofs in geometry and proved the Pythagorean theorem that everybody studies in school.[17] Anaximander (611–547 B.C.) held that living organisms appeared first in water and then passed to dry land, that man was descended from the fish, and that the earth is suspended in space surrounded by heavenly bodies. Anaxagoras (500–428 B.C.) studied the structure of animals by dissection, and Hippocrates (460–377 B.C.) attributed the cause and cure of diseases to natural rather than supernatural phenomena and drafted the Hippocratic Oath which even today sets the ethical standards for medical practitioners.

In the deductive current of thought the first followers of the early Ionians were the Sophists. They were concerned with adult education and taught whoever could pay them. They concentrated their attention upon problems of government and upon methods of argument, and were the founders of dialectics, disputation and the distinguishing of truth from error. They preached that knowledge is not absolute but is relative to man, for example, that good and evil are not absolutes but depend upon man's views. Socrates (469–399 B.C.) reacted strongly against this principle and argued that final knowledge was attainable by reason. His most famous pupil, Plato (427–347 B.C.), endeavoured to deal with this problem of knowledge by stating (he could not prove it) that there are absolutes or super-concepts and that what we observe on earth are mere reflections of these absolutes or super-concepts. Before birth men are acquainted with super-concepts, and knowledge comes by remembering them—a task best performed by the philosopher. This doctrine of "dualism," so-called because what can be known is divided into two parts, has played an important role in Western thought, where it has been used as an argument for the existence of God.

Plato's most famous pupil, Aristotle (384–322 B.C.), attempted to improve on his master's dictum by contending that things of this earth are more than reflections of super-concepts and that from material things we can form generalized concepts, that is, from knowing individual chairs we form a general concept of what constitutes chairs. He thus found God in nature but at the same time brought speculation back to earth. His interests ranged so widely over all manner of things that he has been called the first encyclopaedist. He thought that the earth was spherical in shape and that it was the centre of the universe.[18] He was the founder of the study of biology, of formal logic, of zoology, of botany, and of comparative government. He believed that men were social beings, that they naturally formed States, that the State existed for the well-being of all, and that the moral evolution of man was certain. Aristotle, coming as he did at the extreme end of the middle period, provided a glorious finale to Greece's most brilliant epoch.

Greek civilisation was not, however, able to keep up such high standards, nor were the Greeks capable of maintaining conditions conducive to such great intellectual and artistic achievements. Greece, like so many other famous cultures at their peaks, became the victim of foreign aggression and civil strife. The first important blow came at the beginning of the fifth century B.C., when the country was attacked by Persians. As we have seen previously, these people under Cyrus the Great established a vast empire in the middle of the sixth century and in their territorial expansion over-ran the Greek cities of Asia Minor. Thus Persia came directly into conflict with Greek interests in the Aegean and believed that it could conquer Greece, divided as it was, at will. When the Ionian city of Miletus revolted from Persia and received aid and comfort from mainland Greek cities and especially from Athens, the Persians moved against mainland Greece. Of the ensuing struggle little need be said except that Persia was handicapped by having to wage war overseas, which made the use of its most effective arm—the cavalry—difficult, and by having to meet Greek naval power near its own bases. The first invasion of the Persians was stopped by the Battle of Marathon (490 B.C.) and the second, after the destruction of the city of Athens, by the Battles of Salamis and Plataea (480 B.C. and 479 B.C.).

Yet, saved from one fate, Greece became the victim of another. As so often happens after a victory of allies, the allies soon fell out. Athens, a commercial city, wanted to continue the war against Persia until the Eastern Mediterranean was completely free, but Sparta, an agricultural state, was willing to let well enough alone. To pursue their policy, the Athenians formed an alliance of Aegean and Ionian cities (the Delian League) to carry on the war and actually drove the Persians out of the Aegean. At this point Athens transformed the Delian League into the Athenian Empire and collected payments from her subjects, which were used in part to rebuild Athens (during the Age of Pericles, 461–431 B.C.). At the same time she directed her trade towards the West because of continued Persian and Phoenician hostility in the East. This brought the city immediately into conflict with Corinth, which had had the lion's share of Western business and which feared Athenian supremacy, and with Sparta, which depended on the West for grain. Gradually the opposing positions became solidified, and civil war in Greece ensued— the Peloponnesian War (431–404 B.C.).

This war weakened all the participants, but more important than that it resulted in the triumph of the forces of decentralization within Greece. City-state was embittered against city-state. When Persia demanded the Ionian cities as her reward for financial aid to Sparta, there was no unified Greek will to say her nay. Henceforth the unification of Greek cities of their own free will and accord was impossible. It is a sad commentary that

Greece failed to reconcile the particularism of the city-state with the need for a powerful, unified state. Interests of particular persons, classes, and communities proved more powerful than the general interest. In this fact lay part of Greece's undoing. Inter-city strife continued and was so extensive that of the eighty-five years between the Peloponnesian War and the conquest of Greece by Macedonia, fifty-five years were filled with conflict.

As though this were not bad enough, the general economic position of Greece began to deteriorate. The foreign demand for Greek goods was, relative to the population, declining, for many of those areas that had previously imported Greek goods had learned how to make them, and during the wars had made them. This was particularly noticeable in the Greek cities of Sicily and Magna Graecia and along the southern shores of the Black Sea. Here was a development that was a severe blow to Greece, for it ate away the very foundation upon which her economy was based. Nor were social conditions much better. Unemployment, the fall in real wages, the increase in the debtor class, the influx into the cities of war refugees and adventurers, and the concentration of land-holdings provided fertile soil for popular movements of a revolutionary character. In fact, during the eighty-five years previously mentioned all Greek cities of any size had at least one war or social revolution every ten years. Thus it was that the most brilliant economic and cultural period in Greek history ended in economic depression, political anarchy, and social chaos.

The economy of the Hellenistic Period, 338–30 B.C.

The crisis just described, which confronted Greece in the middle of the fourth century B.C., was of such dimensions as to invite other foreign intervention, this time from Macedonia. This country, which had acquired many Greek techniques and some Greek culture, was united by Philip in the middle of the fourth century B.C. and was soon given by its leader a potent military force composed of small land-holders. This army was organized into solid phalanxes of great striking power, supported by heavy cavalry, bowmen, and corps of engineers equipped with the latest siege weapons devised by Greek scientists. With this force Philip invaded Greece in 338 B.C. and was soon recognized by all but Sparta as leader in the land.

Immediately after Philip's conquest of Greece he effected an alliance of Greek cities to wage war under his leadership against Persia. This was his "great design." He hoped by conquering Persia to remove the most serious threat to his own position and at the same time to effect a unity of the civilised world. The execution of this ambitious plan fell to his son Alexander, later to be known as "the Great," for Philip was murdered as his first contingent of troops was leaving for Asia Minor. At the time Alexander was a mere boy of twenty years, and there were doubts concerning his ability to assume the responsibilities that had come to him. The army was, however, loyal to him and he soon dispelled fears regarding his talents. He defeated the Persians in Asia Minor (334 B.C.); then to protect his flanks and lines of communication, he deprived the Persians of their naval bases in Syria, Phoenicia, and Egypt (333 B.C.); and after a year in Egypt strengthening his position and making certain of food supplies for Greece, he attacked Persian forces in the Mesopotamian plain. In the ensuing campaigns his success was phenomenal—he never lost an engagement from the Hellespont to the Indus River. In 331 B.C. he destroyed the main Persian force near Nineveh and then over-ran all the areas under Persian rule. In 324 B.C. he ascended the Persian throne as "King of the World."

Alexander apparently had plans for developing his newly acquired lands which were almost as ambitious as his dreams of conquest. He did not regard his subjects as mere payers of tribute but as people whose lot could be improved through the exercise of his genius. He founded many cities along Greek lines—including those established by his successors, about three hundred

—which were intended to be economic and cultural centres. He placed Macedonians and Iranians in the chief administrative posts and fostered a policy of fusion between Orientals and Europeans, of which the marriage of his soldiers to natives may be cited as an example. He desired an increase in trade and gave an impetus to it and to a money economy by putting in circulation the hoards of precious metals that he captured.

What Alexander might ultimately have accomplished we do not know, for he died at Babylon in 323 B.C. Immediately his generals began quarrelling over the succession until finally a new series of states, constituted on the basis of a balance-of-power concept, took form. Egypt fell to the Ptolemies, heirs of Lagus, one of Alexander's favourite officers; the East went to Seleucus, a Macedonian nobleman, whose successors were known as the Seleucids; Macedonia and Greece fell to the descendants of Antigonus, a favourite general ; while a few districts remained or soon became independent, notably the compact kingdom of Pergamum in Asia Minor. In general these arrangements were continued until upset by Rome in the second century B.C.

The consequences of Alexander's conquests were so far-reaching that his triumphs have been used to mark a dividing line in the history of antiquity. The Hellenic Period, when the focus was upon the Hellenes and their glorious achievements, now comes to an end, and the Eastern Mediterranean moves into the Hellenistic Period, when attention was centred on the diffusion of Greek techniques, institutions, and culture to the whole of the known world. Indeed the main characteristics of the 200 years after the Macedonian conquest was the triumph of Greek culture over that of the East and the effecting of a unity of culture which had never before been equalled. In this entire process Greece profited less than other areas, because she has the most to give.

Of particular importance to our analysis were foreign borrowings of Greek techniques of production and distribution. In the field of agriculture, for example, Greek methods of husbandry were spread through Greek treatises and were widely practised. The vine and the olive came to be cultivated extensively on a kind of plantation basis. Fertilization and crop rotation were spread. The growing of fodder crops became more general, which tended to make animal raising more a part of settled agriculture and to reduce nomadism on the fringe of arable areas. The irrigation system of Mesopotamia was restored, and in Egypt nearly 500 square miles of good land were reclaimed by further drainage of the Faiyum.

In industry, too, changes following Alexander's conquests were tremendous. Perhaps the most notable effects were on the metal trades, especially iron, because of an increased demand for cheap weapons with which to carry on war and for cheap tools with which to attack nature. Thus an impetus was given to iron production on the south-eastern shore of the Black Sea, in other places in Asia Minor, and in Italy, where the ore of the island of Elba was exploited. Copper mining on Cyprus took a new lease on life, and silver became abundant enough to compete with the finest pottery for tableware. The manufacture of woollens increased in Asia Minor, where there was an abundance of sheep; cotton cloth, first known to the Greeks in the fourth century, was made in Egypt and Phoenicia; and linen and silk were produced on an expanding scale in Egypt and the East. Pergamum became famous for its parchments and Egypt for its papyrus. Ship building developed, particularly at Tyre; the curing of fish, long practised by the Greeks, was adopted by others; and the East generally produced a variety of goods for Mediterranean markets—dyes, bleaching materials, chemicals for paints, asphalt, petroleum, carpets, tapestries, and perfumes.

Trade also developed in the Hellenistic Period, but here again the centres of commerce tended away from mainland Greece. The heyday of Athens and the Piraeus was past, and only Corinth, with its ports on both the Corinthian and Saronic Gulfs, was able to maintain for a time its prominence.[19] Of the Eastern Mediterranean ports Alexandria was one of the most important. As far back as the beginning of the sixth century B.C. Egyptian shipping to the East had grown to a point where an attempt was made to build a canal from the Red Sea to the Nile and Phoenician sailors were sent on a mission to circumnavigate Africa. In time Alexandria became the clearing point for the products of Egypt and for goods obtained along the coasts of the Red Sea, central Africa, and even India. In the Aegean the island of Rhodes, off the south-eastern tip of Asia Minor, was the chief shipping centre for the greater part of the Hellenistic Period, although after the intervention of Rome in the second century B.C. the island of Delos surpassed her for a time. And in the West, commerce centred in Carthage, Syracuse, and ports of central Italy and southern Gaul.

Along the routes of commerce the Greeks gave an impetus to the use of money and banking services. Mints were widely established (the Ptolemies gave Egypt its first currency system), although the Greek drachma was universally recognized as the standard coin. Money-changers put in an appearance, and, as earlier in Greece, they accepted deposits for safe keeping, made loans, transferred funds on their books (Giro banking), and made bottomry loans. With an increase in the size of business enterprises, more funds were sometimes required than could be provided by the savings or borrowings of one man. To meet this situation, partnerships became more frequent, but the device of the joint stock company was probably not hit upon. The increased use of money had also an effect upon public finance. As taxes and tribute came to be paid in money rather than in goods, tax farming was resorted to, that is, the granting to individuals or groups of individuals the right to collect taxes in return for the prior payment to the state of specified sums. This procedure contributed to the development of banking; and so too did the practice of governmental borrowing.

Although the most obvious and most extensive economic consequences of Alexander's conquests were the spread of Greek techniques of production and of Greek business practices, the effects upon Greece itself were of major dimensions. Because of the increase in production abroad, a revival of trade, and a foreign demand for Greek goods at the beginning of the third century B.C., Greece was able for a time to return to her earlier position of being a "work-shop" for others. Her export of goods and earnings from shipping, banking, and giving instruction in the ways of Greece provided a foreign balance which allowed her to import food supplies, raw materials, and luxury goods for the wealthy. Furthermore, economic development in the East and West provided Greeks with alluring opportunities for employment and for investment abroad and led to a new wave of Greek emigration which somewhat relieved the pressure of population at home.

The conquests gave the economy of Greece a shot in the arm —they relieved the economic and social crisis which had confronted Greece in the middle of the fourth century B.C. Unfortunately this return of prosperity was short-lived, for overseas areas, like Rome, began to produce many of those goods formerly obtained from Greece, and trade was hampered by numerous wars between and social disorders within the states of Alexander's empire. As the demand for her goods fell off, Greece was placed in her earlier predicament—a situation that was made still worse by Roman intervention. At the end of the third century B.C., in retaliation for an attempt to upset the balance-of-power system, Rome, now a great power, cut Macedonia off from Greece and the Aegean, isolated Syria, and made Rhodes and Pergamum, both her faithful allies, bases for the preservation of conditions favourable to her. Greece was thereby more effectively deprived of foreign markets and of opportunities for emigration.

Not only did Greece have to face a serious economic situation, but she had also to meet a social crisis of major proportions.

Her population had been increasing steadily and created such a pressure upon the supply of goods that infanticide was widely practised. The trend towards large land-holdings had continued; real wages fell from the peak of post-Alexandrian prosperity; and private debt increased. In all the Greek city-states reform parties clamoured for a re-division of the land, relief from debt, and higher wages. City-states, which were generally governed by the well-to-do, were reluctant to meet such demands, either because, as in Athens, such exceptional sources of revenue as in the mines of Laureion had petered out or because ordinary means of raising funds were limited by poor economic conditions. Although there were instances of city-states furnishing people free amusement and food by gifts or taxes on the rich, there were also many cases of strikes and civil uprisings. Troubles of this kind provided an opportunity for Roman intervention—an intervention that was actively sought by some of the wealthy classes.

In the Hellenized East a not dissimilar economic and social situation developed by the beginning of the second century B.C. Here the age-old concept that the king owned all the land generally prevailed, and in addition the monarchs and their favourites, frequently Greek emigrants, came into possession of the more important industrial and commercial establishments. In Egypt this situation led to an attempt at a centralized control of the economy—to what has been called a "planned economy"; but here as in other areas one thing was certain, the native lower classes benefited little from Hellenization. Wars between the succession states of Alexander's empire diverted energies from productive to destructive ends, impeded trade, and reduced economic activity.

Effective efforts at planned economy degenerated into ostentatious exploitation of the lower classes. Strikes and disorders, sometimes led by priests, were not rare in the second century. In desperation the Ptolemies resorted to inflation (about 170 B.C.) to meet the crisis. In Syria conditions were somewhat better because of trade over the caravan routes, but even here the economy was ailing. Only in the kingdom of Pergamum, extended now to include a large part of Asia Minor, and in Rhodes was there continued prosperity. Yet even in these places the future was not bright. Rome did not want its satellites to develop to a point where they might be politically dangerous, and the time came when both of these states were accused of treason and punished (about 168 B.C.).

All efforts to free Greece or other parts of the East from Roman interference only resulted in disastrous wars and eventual defeat. Indeed, the chief characteristic of economic history of the Eastern Mediterranean in the last two centuries B.C. was the gradual absorption of the area into the orbit of the Roman empire. Once again the economic centre of gravity was moving westward—this time to the Italian peninsula.

As the economies of other areas came to surpass the material well-being of Greece, so too intellectual and artistic accomplishments came to be of a higher order in those places of the Mediterranean that were being Hellenized than in Greece itself. Cities like Athens surrendered leadership to Ephesus, Pergamum, Rhodes, Antioch, and above all to Alexandria in Egypt. The avid desire for learning in these places is apparent from schools established in the Athenian tradition and from the formation of great libraries, of which that of Alexandria was the greatest with 500,000 rolls, most of which were Greek. In the new and growing urban centres there was of necessity a great amount of building which provided opportunities for Greek artists that were not to be found in mainland Greece. Here we see Greeks engaged in city planning, in building Corinthian structures of both a public and a private character, and in decorating these buildings with sculpture and painting. Much of this work was of great excellence, as for example the statue of the "Dying Gaul" at Pergamum, "Laocoon" and the "Victory of Samothrace" at Rhodes, and "Venus of Milo" of the Alexandrian school. Yet the introduction

THE HELLENISTIC WORLD

MILES
0   100   200   300

palacios

of the arch began to make architecture more massive, statues were frequently of the colossal type, and painting, now paying more attention to landscape, became more ornate.

In literature creative work was less distinctive and powerful than it had been in fifth-century Greece. Tragedy died out, and the comedy of Aristophanes was supplanted by "the new comedy" of character and intrigue.[20] The mime, diatribe, and idyll were common, but most writing was in prose.[21] Here we find dull chronicles, histories, historical fiction, and travel tales, usually inspired by Alexander's exploits. In philosophy less attention was given to great cosmological, metaphysical, and epistemological questions than to emotional aspects of religion and to ethical escapism. This may have been because in the East the vast number of uprooted and poor people needed some rationalization of their misery.[22]

Already in fifth-century Greece, mystery cults had developed which preached that a knowledge of God could not be attained by the senses but rather by meditation, intuition, asceticism, or spells of ecstasy, that religion purifies the soul, and that a purified soul could get its rewards in heaven. These beliefs in the East were elaborated with a priesthood, initiation rights, sacramental meals, messiahs, powers of healing, virgin births, rituals, and symbols. Thus Greece and the East developed a whole body of religious practices which made progress in the West in the second century B.C. and some of which were adopted by the later Christians.

It was, however, in science that the greatest achievements of the Hellenistic Period were realized. In many of the Eastern cities, but especially in Alexandria with its observatory and medical school, the knowledge of Babylonia, Egypt, and Greece was fused for later transmission to the West. In general there was a trend away from speculation and system-making to actual observation and investigation. Yet for the most part research was of a theoretical rather than of an immediately practical character. Perhaps the most notable work of the period was in mathematics, for at that time Euclid published his *Elements* (about 300 B.C.), Apollonius of Perga (247–205 B.C.) prepared his geometry of cones, Hipparchus (160–125 B.C.) invented plane and spherical trigonometry, and only a little later Hero of Alexandria (50 B.C.), who built the first "steam engine"—a toy pin-wheel run by steam from a tea-kettle spout—worked out the algebraic formula for a number of areas and volumes.

In this period, too, there were astronomers who held that the earth rotates on its axis every twenty-four hours,[23] who suggested that the sun rather than the earth is the centre of the Universe,[24] and who made elaborate categories of heavenly bodies.[25] In medicine, Herophilus of Chalcedon (about 300 B.C.), the "father" of anatomy, named the upper portion of the intestines "duodenum," the place where the most fashionable ulcers of our time are found, and Erasistratus (about 290 B.C.), the father of physiology, distinguished between sensory and motor nerves and gave the valves of the heart the names used today. In geography, the size of the earth was computed almost exactly, the concept of latitude and longitude was established, and the climatic zones were named. In physics and engineering, Archimedes of Syracuse (287–212 B.C.) arrived at an almost exact value for π, developed hydrostatics, and explained the principles of the lever, compound pulley, endless screw, and burning mirror.

The Hellenistic Period was obviously not barren of important cultural advance towards a fuller understanding of the world— an understanding that was essential for a more extensive control of that world by humankind. Yet in this period, it should be noted again, the best work was done in the Eastern cities, which became the crossroads of trade and thought, and in the century of this area's greatest economic prosperity. Here once more is evidence of a correlation between cultural and intellectual achievement and economic progress—a correlation that we found in the history of mainland Greece, of Egypt, of Babylonia, and of Sumer. We have witnessed again the role which the process of borrowing from others has played in the development of civilisation, of the importance of conditions which allow individuals to realize freely and fully their potential talents, of the predicaments in which people are placed if their economies fail to keep pace in production with the growth of population, and of the curse of such disintegrating forces as social strife and war. When peoples become weak economically, socially, and politically, they fall prey to others. Such was the case of Greece and the East when the Romans came.

FOOTNOTES TO CHAPTER IV

1 These wars are believed to have occurred between 1194 and 1184 B.C. Archaeologists have identified nine cities on the site of Troy for the period between Neolithic and Greco-Roman times. The dates assigned to the seventh city, of which Homer sang, are 1350 B.C. and 1184 B.C.

2 Thracians moved into Asia Minor, forcing the Phrygians into the Anatolian highlands, Lydians into the south-western corner of Asia Minor, the Philistines to the Syrian coastal plain, and peoples who were to be known as Etruscans to the Italian peninsula north of Rome.

3 Much of our knowledge concerning the agriculture of this period comes from Hesiod, *Works and Days*, written about 735 B.C.

4 In this connection we should mention that the Sophists in the fifth century B.C. preached the doctrine of the "supremacy of the individual," that is, that the welfare of the individual was to have precedence over all other considerations.

5 Incidentally, reduction in the cost of iron compared with bronze allowed members of the lower classes to possess weapons with which they could advance their interests with force.

6 In time the Greeks realized that the depletion of the forests was making them short of timber and was resulting in soil erosion. They then attempted reafforestation but had only a moderate success.

7 William L. Westermann, "Greek Culture and Thought," *Encyclopædia of the Social Sciences*, The Macmillan Company, New York, 1937, Vol. I, p. 20.

8 The most dramatic example was the reconstruction of Athens under the direction of Pericles following the Persian Wars, that is, about 461 to

431 B.C. This enterprise, which involved the construction of the Parthenon and other buildings on the Acropolis, led to the employment of one of Greece's greatest architects, Ictinus, and one of her great sculptors, Phidias.

9 An early landmark was Myron's "Discus Thrower" of about 450 B.C.

10 See the works of Phidias in the fifth century B.C.

11 These qualities are visible in the work of Praxiteles, fourth century B.C., and of Scopas, a contemporary.

12 Among the better known are Sappho of Lesbos (about 600 B.C.) and Pindar (522–448 B.C.).

13 Among the tragedies should be mentioned those of Aeschylus (525–456 B.C.), Sophocles (496–406 B.C.), and Euripides (480–406 B.C.). Among the comedies the most distinguished were those of Aristophanes (448–388 B.C.).

14 This was true of Herodotus (484–425 B.C.). He attempted a universal account of the past of known Asiatic peoples and of the deeds of the Greeks and Persians in the Persian Wars.

15 This was the case of Thucydides (465–396 B.C.) who wrote of the Peloponnesian War. He was the most careful workman and the most penetrating analyst among the Greek historians.

16 Xenophon (430–354 B.C.) illustrates this tendency. He was a student of rhetoric, the art of writing and speaking with grace and ease. The Athenian orator Demosthenes (384–322 B.C.) was an eminent rhetorician.

17 For those who may have forgotten, it can be restated thus: In a right-angle triangle the square of the hypotenuse is equal to the sum of the squares of the other two sides.

18 This is the geocentric theory as opposed to the heliocentric theory, that the sun is the centre of the universe.

19 Corinth was burned by the Romans in 146 B.C., but it was revived by Julius Caesar and Augustus.

20 Menander (342–291 B.C.) was perhaps the leading writer of this school.

21 The last Greek epic was by Apollonius of Rhodes (about 194 B.C.), who wrote on the well-worn theme of Jason and the Golden Fleece.

22 The five important ethical schools were as follows: (1) The Cynic, whose most important thinker was Diogenes of Sinope (412–323 B.C.) and whose main programme included attacks upon social institutions, particularly on private property. (2) The Cyrenaic, which preached the pursuit of pleasure. (3) The Sceptic, led by Pyrrho (360–270 B.C.), which taught that unhappiness results from an inability to attain knowledge and that one should therefore renounce all efforts to attain it. (4) The Stoic, whose master was Zeno (336–264 B.C.), which held that God is good, that man should live according to the law of God, and that if one were unfortunate, one should bear up like a man. (5) Epicurean, whose leader was Epicurus (341–270 B.C.), which

contended that the end of life is pleasure but that this pursuit should be avoided if it caused pain.

23 Heraclides of Pontus (388–315 B.C.).

24 Aristarchus (310–230 B.C.). He also computed accurately the distance from the earth to the moon.

25 Hipparchus (160–125 B.C.). He elaborated the geocentric theory and the theory of epicycles to explain the movement of the planets, moon and sun—a theory which was not upset until modern times. He also used the Babylonian system of dividing the circle into 360 degrees for purposes of observation, and he is said to have invented an astrolabe.

For Further Reading

Cambridge Ancient History (1923–1939), 12 Vols.

Benjamin Farrington, *Science in Antiquity* (1936)

H. N. Fowler, *A History of Ancient Greek Literature* (1923)

F. M. Heichelheim, *Wirtschaftsgeschichte des Altertums* (1938), 2 Vols.

A. H. M. Jones, *The Greek City from Alexander to Justinian* (1940)

M. L. Laistner, *Greek History* (1932)

R. W. Livingstone, *The Legacy of Greece* (1924)

M. Rostovtzeff, *The Social and Economic History of the Hellenistic World* (1941), 3 Vols.

W. W. Tarn, *Hellenistic Civilisation* (1927)

J. Toutain, *The Economic Life of the Ancient World* (1930)

H. B. Walker, *Art of the Greeks* (1922)

William L. Westermann, "Greek Culture and Thought," *Encyclopaedia of the Social Sciences* (1937), Vol. I

V

ROME

ALTHOUGH Greece had lost its economic, political, and cultural vitality by the end of the Hellenistic Period, many of the seeds of its culture had taken root and were to flower in the Italian peninsula, whence, altered by local conditions, they were to spread again, especially in Western Europe. Indeed, the significance of Roman culture in world history is derived from the fact that it effected a new synthesis of Greek culture, added to it certain developments of its own, and through the process of diffusion provided fundamental elements in the culture of the people from the eastern Balkans to Poland and from Finland to the Mediterranean, as well as of the people in all parts of the globe colonized by Western Europeans.[1] It was from Rome that these people obtained to a large extent their religion, their state system, parts of their law, basic intellectual concepts, forms of art, and their emphasis on material welfare.

The place of Roman culture in world history

The diffusion of Roman culture is not, however, the object of our immediate interest. Rather we are concerned once again with those factors that allowed this culture to create an economic surplus and with the question whether or not there was correspondence between economic well-being, on the one hand, and satisfactory social arrangements and the production of works of a high intellectual and artistic quality, on the other. In the pages that follow we shall see how Rome ultimately conquered all the known world, how she exchanged her industrial products for raw materials and foodstuffs, and how she succeeded in acquiring large deliveries of tribute from conquered peoples. Rome prospered most when her commerce and her collections of tribute were at their maximum, that is, in the first century B.C. and in the first two centuries of the Christian Era. Her period of highest civilisation was also in these same centuries. Afterwards, Rome failed to produce a vigorous and original intellectual life or to create forms of artistic expression able to stand the critical test of time.

Because Roman development was so dependent upon conquest, Roman history may be divided most usefully into segments for study according to the extent to which Rome exercised her dominion over others. Thus the first period reaches from the Bronze Age, through the establishment of an Iron Age economy and policy, to the time when Rome had conquered all the Italian peninsula, that is, from about 1000 to approximately 270 B.C. The second period extends from 270 B.C. to A.D. 14—a period in which Rome triumphed over Carthage, Spain, Cisalpine Gaul, Greece, Macedonia, Transalpine Gaul, all North Africa, Egypt, Syria, Palestine, and parts of Asia Minor. The third period covers the first and second centuries A.D., in which Rome expanded over all the territory from the British Isles to the Caspian Sea and the Tigris River and from beyond the Rhine and Danube Rivers to the African deserts. The fourth period, from the end of the second century to the sixth century A.D., is characterized by Rome's loss of authority throughout the Empire, by foreign or barbarian invasions, and by the creation of small, independent states even in the Italian peninsula itself.

As the rise of Rome is to be explained largely through superior techniques of production and trade and through conquests, so too the fall of Rome is to be accounted for largely by the loss of particular advantages of industry and commerce and by the political disintegration of the Empire. In the course of time Rome taught its techniques to people in areas more richly endowed with natural resources than she; her labour force, supported by "bread and circuses," came to care little for work; and her capitalist class tended to spend its surplus on luxuries rather than to invest it in productive equipment. Conquered areas resented being eternally milked by Rome, and a time finally came when they refused or were unable longer to supply Rome with goods needed to sustain life. Rome's wealthy ruling class fought over spoils to be had from the peninsula or the Empire and became too divided and too soft for imperial management. When the Roman Empire fell apart in a general wave of economic, political, and social disorganization, the Roman world, with the exception of Byzantium, had little vitality left, and it entered the dark ages of the early Medieval Period.

Beginnings of Roman power, 1000 to 270 B.C.

That Rome had to rely so heavily upon goods from its Empire in order to attain its high economic position is to be explained in part by geographical factors. The Italian peninsula, which has from time immemorial been aptly described as resembling the shape of a boot, is not richly endowed with natural resources. It is predominantly mountainous, with the Alps at the north being continued by the Apennines, which run from the top of the boot to the arch and under another name even to the very toe. Arable land is found primarily in the Po plain, along the coasts, and in the mountain valleys, and is limited to about one-third of the entire surface of the peninsula. In general, then, the land of Italy is analogous to that of Greece, although it is four times larger.

In spite of limited arable land, Italy had in ancient times certain geographical assets which were conducive to economic development. At the beginning of the first millennium B.C. its mountains were well forested and ready to supply an abundance of timber for building and charcoal. Its foothills and sea marshes provided good pasturage. Its copper and iron deposits, particularly iron ore on the island of Elba, could be worked without great difficulty. In common with other ancient cultures it had excellent means of water transportation, and, being located near the centre of the Mediterranean, it could easily get part of the trade between the highly developed Eastern Mediterranean and the unexploited West. Finally, although it was relatively safe from the concerted attacks of its neighbours, it could deploy forces in all directions.

Undoubtedly, also, the geographical position of the Italian peninsula had much to do with the fact that migratory peoples from several cultures went there as colonizers and that they were able to maintain contact with, and hence borrow steadily from, many sources. Towards the end of the second millennium B.C. there arrived in Italy a people from the Danube Valley, who brought with them knowledge of the use of iron. They were followed a little later by the Etruscans from Asia Minor, who imported their Eastern techniques and culture to the district north of the Tiber. Theirs was a policy of expansion, but in the sixth century B.C. they were stopped in the Po Valley by another invading people, the Celts. Then from the middle of the eighth century B.C. came Greeks who colonized the district southward from Naples, in the area which came to be known as Great Greece. Thus like Greece, Rome inherited from various cultures its productive techniques and much of its transmissible knowledge.

When the Etruscans arrived in the peninsula, the existing tribes were practising settled agriculture, were making textile, bronze, and iron products, and must have been engaged in trade, for tin in the bronze had to come from afar. In spite of these evidences of economic progress, the Etruscans effected a real change in the economic life of Italy. They knew much about drainage and irrigation, and before long they had made such swampy areas as the Tuscan Maremma, the Roman Campagna, and the Pontine Marshes fertile and healthy areas. They built embankments along the Po to control that river, and they constructed the famous drainage canal, the Cloaca Maxima, near Rome's Palatine Hill, which furnished a model for the recovery of swampy land in the city. They increased agricultural production, which made possible the rise of cities, and the rise of cities led to the growth of industries. The Etruscans opened quarries for their buildings; they began mining in Tuscany and Elba, and they gave an impetus to the making of pottery on the wheel. Furthermore, they carried on trade with Greece, Phoenicia, Carthage, and Greek colonies in southern Italy. In brief, they developed an economy which made possible the accumulation of considerable economic surplus.

From the Etruscans the neighbouring native tribes learned much, but the people of Latium were the ones to take fullest advantage of what they had learned. Their city of Rome grew into a commercial centre and for a time was the seat of Etruscan power in Italy. Ultimately the people of Rome succeeded in freeing themselves from their erstwhile teachers, the last of the Etruscan kings, the Tarquins, being expelled from Rome at the end of the sixth century B.C. Then Rome, strengthened internally by the institution of a republican form of government which lasted until near the end of the first century B.C., began the conquest of the peninsula. By 270 B.C. Rome was in control of all the territory from the Straits of Messina, which separate Sicily and the mainland, to somewhat north of Pisa. The conquests had two important consequences in so far as Rome's status was concerned: first, they brought her into conflict with the powerful Greek state of Epirus, which sought to defend its interests in Great Greece; and second, they encroached upon the Carthaginian sphere of influence in Sicily. The defeat of Epirus made the world realize that Rome was a major power, while victory over Carthage in the ensuing period was to lead Rome on the path of foreign expansion, of overseas trade, and of collecting tribute from conquered peoples.

The economic surplus that Rome had to devote to war during the conquest of the peninsula resulted primarily from the use of Etruscan and Greek techniques. Then, as new lands were conquered, individual Romans got more land to which they could apply their technology, and the Roman world acquired the means of obtaining great revenue. A part of the conquered lands was given to favoured individuals; a part, the "public land," was leased to patricians or to wealthy plebeians; and a part was left with former owners in return for a substantial payment. Money that went to the Roman treasury helped to finance further expansion, while lands that fell to Roman citizens allowed the building of great personal fortunes.

Some of the accumulated capital was invested in industry and commerce, and both these branches of economic activity expanded during the wars for conquest of the peninsula. The need for military equipment stimulated metal-working and arms manufacture. The construction of great roads, for which Rome was to become famous, was begun—the Appian Way to the south and south-east, the Latin and Flaminian Ways to the east and north-east, and the Aurelian Way to the north-west—and because of them goods began to move overland in greater quantities. Trade with Greece and North Africa also grew, and Rome acquired at least a small merchant fleet of its own, although its range of action was limited by treaties with Carthage and other cities to the Tyrrhenian Sea. Finally, about the middle of the fourth century Rome established a coinage system—a sure sign of growing commercial activity.

In the first period of Roman history, from 1000 to 270 B.C., there was, then, considerable economic expansion, the amassing of surplus as is evidenced by the conduct of wars, and the concentration of a certain amount of wealth in the hands of craftsmen, patricians, and merchants. How much of this surplus was used for intellectual or artistic enterprise in the very early history of Rome we do not know. From what knowledge we have of the formative period of Rome's culture, it appears that more attention was given then to the extension of control over physical and human environment than to intellectual and artistic activity.

Of particular interest was the establishment of institutions that gave all citizens a sense of civic responsibility, ambition for individual material betterment, and rules for the conduct of basic human relations. An important factor in the development of the Roman pattern of behaviour was the requirement, established under the stress of military exigency, that all land-holding citizens between the ages of seventeen and sixty-five were liable for military service and for the cost of their own equipment. This drafting of the lower classes for military service was accompanied by reforms that gave the *plebs* a greater voice in government. Their members were given full citizenship,[2] were permitted to aspire to the highest offices in the state, could participate in the most important political decisions, could make laws by the early third century B.C. by means of *plebiscita*, and possessed in the Tribunes personal advocates of their own causes. Thus they came to feel that the welfare of Rome depended to a large extent on them; that they could improve their own lot; and that personal betterment was highly desirable.

Nevertheless, the *plebs* did not become political masters in Rome, nor was there any important levelling movement. In actual practice, the *plebs* elected patricians to the chief offices, and the Senate curbed the rights of the Tribunes by refusing advancement to those who proved obstreperous. Hence what was in form a representative republic was in actuality an oligarchy of the wealthy.[3] The Laws of the Twelve Tables, established about 450 B.C. and for long basic in Roman society, protected private property and facilitated capital formation by regularizing the transfer of property.[4] Under the existing system Romans could and did amass fortunes which helped finance the advancement of Roman civilisation.

Rome becomes a world power, 270 B.C.–A.D. 14

In the formative period of Roman culture a desire for economic progress, ambition for personal material improvement, and a tendency towards the orderly conduct of relations among citizens of the state were clearly established. In the next period of Roman history, from 270 B.C. to A.D. 14, the last of these goals was for a time not realized, but the former ideologies found expression in the great wars of Roman expansion—wars that effected important changes in Roman culture. In these two and a half centuries Rome fought Carthage, Macedonia, Syria, Greece, and Egypt and conducted campaigns against native tribes in northern Italy, Spain, and southern Gaul. Although there were moments when Roman armies were sorely pressed, they emerged in the end victors over all their enemies. By the beginning of the Christian Era Rome had conquered most of the Mediterranean and was easily the greatest power in existence.

Of all the wars that Rome waged after 270 B.C. the three against Carthage were the most crucial to her development and to the future of the world.[5] They launched her on a policy of expansion outside the Italian peninsula; they inaugurated her policy of collecting tribute and otherwise of attempting to live off conquered people; and they determined whether Greco-Roman or Phoenician-Carthaginian culture was to be predominant in the West.

Rome became embroiled with Carthage by supporting the time-honoured policies of the Greek cities of southern Italy to expand their commercial activities in areas dominated by Carthage and by threatening Carthaginian interests in Sicily. In the wars that followed, Carthage proved to be a formidable foe, and the outcome was not certain until the end. Carthage had a great potential for war, based upon the successful development of agriculture in North Africa, upon industries within her cities, and, most characteristic of all, upon an extensive commerce.[6]

Furthermore, the Carthaginians had a powerful fleet, a cavalry superior to that of the Romans, a knowledge of all the Hellenistic machines of war, mercenaries schooled in Hellenistic methods of warfare, and a force of elephants, which, like the modern heavy tank, was used to break through enemy lines. Yet, in spite of their strength, the Carthaginians were at last defeated. They were handicapped by having to do much of their fighting overseas and by having mercenary soldiers who, unlike the Roman citizen-soldier, lacked staying power in moments of crisis.

That Rome was able to overcome such a strong adversary speaks well for its economic strength. Even though the wars were costly in men and resources and though Italy was a battleground for twelve long years in the Second Punic War and was ravaged by Carthaginians under the brilliant leadership of Hannibal, the Italian peninsula experienced a movement towards further urbanization and industrialization. With the influx of capital from defeated countries, there was investment in new industrial enterprise. With labour moving from the country to towns, there was a greater working force available for domestic manufacture. And with the growth of cities, particularly of Rome, which became the largest city in the known world,[7] there was an increased demand for industrial products.

Urbanization stimulated the building trades and allied fields like quarrying, brick-making, and the supply of timber. The construction of aqueducts to supply cities with water gave a fillip to stone-masonry, engineering, and plumbing, as in the manufacture and installation of lead pipes for the distribution of water to public fountains and individual buildings. Industry and war created a demand for iron and bronze tools and weapons. In Campania, the town of Puteoli, the modern Pozzuoli, became a centre for the production of spears, javelins, swords, picks, scythes, and chisels, while Capua specialized in kitchen utensils, especially the ubiquitous pots and pans. During the first century B.C. the famous Arretine earthenware, which came to supply a large part of the West with better grades, was established. Then there were also jewellery-making, gold-working, leather-working, ship-building, and a host of other important trades.

For the most part industrial production was concentrated in small workshops of the handicraft type, but some was conducted upon large estates, where baskets, rough crocks, and tables were made and where frequently olives and grapes were put through presses. Some industry was established by *entrepreneurs* on a relatively large scale, especially in the case of mining, quarrying, brick-making, and metal-working. At all events, a division of labour took place which greatly increased output. We find specialized free workers organizing *collegia*, a kind of benefit society, on the basis of their trades. Thus by the end of the Republic, Rome had a thriving industry. Yet Roman culture had produced little in the way of new techniques, made almost no use of non-human energy, and did not tap inorganic matter as a source of power. Its inability to advance technically placed definite limits upon its industrial expansion.

The wars between 270 B.C. and A.D. 14 also effected changes in Roman agriculture which were as significant for Rome's welfare as changes in its industry. In the first place, there was a trend towards the concentration of landholdings. The well-to-do acquired large estates—the *latifundia*—by purchase or lease,[8] while the poorer farmers frequently sold their holdings and moved to the cities or became agricultural labourers or small tenants. In the early period, as we have seen, landholders were required to perform military service without pay and were called to arms at any and all times of the year. In such circumstances the small landholder was at a tremendous disadvantage, for he was not in a position to get someone to carry on his work while he was away. If he were killed in battle, no one might be available to till his acres, and they would have to be sold. If he did return from the war with a whole skin, his fields would most likely be unkempt, his livestock driven away, and his buildings in disrepair.

The poor returning veteran frequently felt that the sale of his land was the best way out of his predicament.

Henceforth in Roman history the question of large holdings was a serious one, but all attempts at reform, of which those sponsored by the brothers Tiberius and Gaius Grachus were the most famous (133–123 B.C.), proved abortive. To provide labour for the great estates, owners employed not only landless freemen but, on a mounting scale, slaves from the Eastern slave markets and from captives taken in war. With the introduction of slave labour on the large farms, Italian agriculture underwent a profound change. Large landholders turned from the growing of grain to the cultivation of the olive and the vine and to the raising of livestock. So important did these branches of agriculture become that behind the plea of Cato, himself a landowner, for the destruction of Carthage was the hope that Carthaginian competition in oil and wine would be wiped out.[9]

With concentration on the growing of olives and grapes large landholders let drainage works fall into disuse and the land that had been reclaimed to return to malarial swamp, a condition that has only been rectified in recent times. Furthermore, Rome became dependent upon foreign imports for a significant part of its food supply, a situation that necessitated control of foreign areas to assure regular deliveries and that led to governmental sale of grain at a low price—to a policy of bread for the poor.[10]

Perhaps the outstanding economic consequence of Rome's foreign conquests was the enormous growth of trade. Now Rome dominated a large portion of the known world, and trade followed the flag. Improvements were made to such ports as Puteoli, the chief shipping centre on the Tyrrhenian Sea, to Ostia, at the mouth of the Tiber and the port of Rome, to Brindisi, to Utica, and to many others. Roman roads were established throughout the peninsula, and new ones were constructed through southern Gaul from the Alps to the Pyrenees and across northern Greece from the Adriatic to the Aegean. Caravan routes in the Near East were improved, and at Rome itself the commercial district around the Aventine Hill was greatly expanded.

With the development of trade the Italian peninsula received more and more goods of all kinds from every point of the compass. From Sicily, North Africa, and the East came grain. From Gaul and Spain came copper, silver, lead, tin, wool, and hides. From the East came spices, perfumes, and carpets. From the Black Sea came salt fish. From Asia Minor came cloth and dyestuffs. And from Greece were brought in works of art and other luxuries. For these imports Italy could not export goods of equal value, although she did sell abroad metallurgical products, wool, timber, naval supplies, and pottery. The balance of trade in goods was usually against her, but her deficit in goods was more than covered by tribute in kind or money and by the earnings on Roman property held abroad.[11]

Redressing the trade balance in this manner raises the question of Rome's exploitation of her foreign territories. As we have already seen, Rome began with the First Punic War to demand tribute from conquered regions, initiating the policy to help meet the heavy debts incurred during the conflict and continuing it because of its lucrative nature. Tribute might be in the form of a portion of a grain harvest, royalties on mining, customs duties, income from lands either sold or rented, and seizures of precious metals from treasuries and temples. To the sums thus obtained should be added booty that was taken at random by the military and the income which favourite Roman citizens realized on property that they acquired overseas.

For the most part tribute was collected by tax farmers. Tax farming had come into being prior to the Roman expansion outside Italy, when the collection of taxes and rents, the provisioning of the army, and the handling of all governmental expenditures had been auctioned off to the highest bidder. As Rome began its conquests of foreign areas, the system was simply extended. In many cases the tax farmers conducted their affairs without honesty, pity, or scruples of any kind, and they amassed large amounts of capital. Nor, as a rule, did the governors of the provinces attempt to rectify matters. On the contrary they often followed the examples set by the tax farmers and exploited their charges without mercy. Many of the officials, like Pompey, Crassus, Antonius, and Caesar, were able to create great personal fortunes which they could use for investment and for furthering their own political ambitions.

Through foreign trade, tribute collecting, and tax farming, Rome developed its major institutions for facilitating capital accumulation and investment. The tax farmers, known as "publicans," had money to lend. So too did money-changers, who profited from laws requiring foreign traders to change their coins to Roman.[12] And so also did shippers, who frequently financed the cargoes that they carried. So there developed such practices as the receipt of money for deposit, the transfer of funds, the acceptance of bills of exchange, trading in shares of companies, loans, and the sale of annuities. Probably bankers lent money principally for productive enterprise, but they also made loans for consumption, helped finance ambitious persons like Caesar, and assisted Eastern cities in meeting their obligations. Although the maximum legal rate of interest was 12 per cent., established in the Twelve Tables of about 450 B.C. and thereafter frequently reiterated, rates for non-productive and risky ventures ran as high as 48 per cent. per annum. Furthermore, rates fluctuated widely, for the supply of money varied sharply as Rome brought in new quantities of precious metals from a campaign or failed for a long time to do so. And because Rome had to import so much grain, poor crops necessitated large purchases abroad that drained off money. Hence Rome had business fluctuations due to agricultural conditions and the amount of money obtained in conquest.[13]

Although Rome did a poor job of regulating the supply of

money in order to minimize swings in business activity, she made one important contribution to business organization in creating the joint stock company. This institution came into being as a result of tax farming. When Rome made important conquests abroad and demanded very large sums in return for the privilege of collecting taxes for the state and provisioning troops, it sometimes happened that no one individual had sufficient funds to make the advance payment. Hence publicans banded together to take "shares" in the enterprise and offered other shares to the investing public, particularly to senators who were prohibited by law from participating directly in tax farming. There thus came into being an exceptionally important method for harnessing capital from many sources for speculative trading in shares of business enterprise.

As a whole the two and a half centuries of Roman history prior to the birth of Christ witnessed an enormous economic development, not only in total goods available for consumption in Italy and growth of population but also in goods available per capita of the population. Rome established important economic institutions for the accumulation and investment of capital, developed its own industrial capacity, greatly extended its trade, and altered the character of its agriculture. Rome was thus able to add to the resources of the Italian peninsula by tapping supplies from other areas, to increase production by a division of labour and by allowing various localities in the Empire to specialize in those things for which they were best suited, and to amass wealth that could be used for development of the arts and sciences.

Perhaps the greatest weakness of Roman civilisation at this time was the lack of harmonious human relations. In fact, so great was the hostility among social classes and aspirants to political power that Rome's exalted position was threatened. Among the more important elements in the situation were: (1) there were the former small landowners who had been pushed off their holdings and who felt resentment towards large proprietors; (2) there were slaves who were treated poorly and who were antagonistic towards their masters; (3) there were the poor plebeians who felt that they were exploited by the wealthy and who were not content with "bread-and-circus" policies; (4) there were the *equites*, or knights, rich tradesmen, industrialists, and tax farmers, who were jealous of the patrician class; (5) there were the senators, who held the real political power of the state and had the greatest prestige, but who were not necessarily the richest, as they were excluded from such profitable businesses as tax farming and shipping; and finally (6) there were the military men and high state officials who reaped large profit from their services and who frequently nourished extravagant ambitions.

During the early life of the Republic, political differences between plebeians and patricians were resolved by concessions and compromise. Now such a happy solution was not found, and from 125 to 27 B.C. Rome was afflicted by domestic strife initiated in the interest of some class or pressure group or combinations of classes or groups. The details of these internal struggles are exceedingly complicated and need not be repeated here. The chief facts to remember are that slaves and plebeians got little from their uprisings and that ultimately the struggle was among senators, knights, and commanders of various Roman armies who fought for control of the state in the hope of being able to reap the largest share of the spoils. It was this situation that gave rise to the meteoric careers of men like Pompey, Antonius, and Caesar—and which led in many cases to their violent ends.

This state of affairs could not be allowed to continue, for if Italy was devastated by civil war and if Roman armies fought one another to impotence, foreign provinces of the Empire might revolt and become independent of Rome's authority. Obviously no one in his right mind wanted to kill a goose while she was laying golden eggs. Finally, Octavius Caesar, better known by his title of Augustus, a grandnephew of Julius Caesar, restored order and was made *Princeps civitatis*—the first citizen of the state—a title that he held from 31 B.C. to A.D. 14 and which gave to his regime and that of his early successors the name of Principate. Augustus set about the re-establishment of Roman authority and governmental machinery so that Italy could continue to draw upon the production of the foreign provinces. This basic policy appealed to contesting Roman factions, and Augustus strove to carry it out with a strong but diplomatic hand. He curbed the power of the Senate but pacified its members by allowing them to retain their social privileges and rights to certain posts. He paid government officials so well that graft, now punished severely, was reduced to a minimum. He abolished tax farming, yet won the support of the knights by giving them certain privileges and by restoring peace and order for the conduct of business. He won the *plebs* by hand-outs of free grain and free entertainment on a scale more lavish than that of Caesar himself. He secured the support of foreign provinces by the restoration of order and by stopping predatory tax farmers and governors. And he minimized the possibility of military commanders rising against established authority by making them responsible to him, changing them frequently, and placing them and their armies on the frontiers where danger threatened.[14]

The reforms of Augustus were of the utmost importance to the future of Rome and of the ancient world. First, they effected a different kind of control over human environment than had existed previously and one that greatly restricted individual action. The Republic was in essence abolished, for the new rulers assumed extensive personal powers which were given legal form when the Empire came into being towards the close of the first century A.D. Second, the policies of Augustus effected a compromise among social classes which perpetuated the existing class structure and thus permitted the upper classes, particularly the knights, to continue to enjoy a dominant position in society

ROMAN CULTURE

BARBARIAN INVASIONS

GOTHS ⟶
HUNS ⟶
ANGLO-SAXONS ⟶
VANDALS, SUEVI, FRANKS ⟶

Caspian Sea

TIGRIS R.
EUPHRATES R.
Ctesiphon
Antioch
SYRIA
PALESTINE
Alexandria
Caesarea
EGYPT
palacios

Black Sea
Sinope
Pergamum
Byzantium
Athens
Mediterranean Sea
CYRENAICA

Dacia
DANUBE
Vienna
ILLYRIA

Cologne
Paris
GAUL
Lyons
Bordeaux

BRITANNIA
London

Massilia
Ravenna
Naples
Rome
Ostia
Carthage
SPAIN
Toledo
Cadiz
MAURETANIA

MILES
0   200   500

and in politics. Third, and most happily for Rome, Augustus prevented a disintegration of the conquered areas comparable to that of the Empire of Alexander the Great. He and his followers in the first two centuries A.D. succeeded in maintaining relative peace within and among the parts of Rome's vast holdings. Pax Romana, based to a large degree on force, made possible the turning of energies to peace-time production. As a result, all the Empire enjoyed relatively good economic conditions for nearly two centuries.

The greatest flowering of Roman culture is usually said to have been in the first century B.C., and in this period achievements in the arts, particularly in literature and architecture, began to rival accomplishments in politics, law, and engineering. It was then that Greek influence on Roman culture was everywhere apparent. Following Rome's victories over Great Greece, Carthage, and Greece, Greek ambassadors, hostages, craftsmen, traders, artists, and scholars began to flock to the banks of the Tiber and there to turn out their kind of products. Things Greek were in fashionable demand in Rome, Romans of "distinction" believing that they must know the Greek language and Greek culture. Attempts to satisfy the demand appeared on every hand. In literature we find that Livius Andronicus (about 284–204 B.C.) translated the *Odyssey*; Ennius (about 239–169 B.C.), the "father of Latin literature," wrote a historical epic of Rome in Greek hexameters and composed Latin comedies and tragedies using Greek models; Polybius (about 204–122 B.C.) wrote in Greek a history of the Punic Wars; and Terence (about 190–159 B.C.) produced works after the new Greek comedy. In architecture, the Romans adopted the Greek temple with its colonnaded porch and enclosed *cella*, simply placing the structure upon a raised foundation (*podium*). In painting and sculpture, Romans sought Greek works for decorating their buildings and immortalizing themselves. So highly, indeed, did the Romans hold Greek culture that they adopted Greek gods, giving them Roman names,[15] and endeavoured through the creation of the Trojan War legend regarding the origin of Latium to trace their ancestry to Greek sources.

Although the first century B.C. witnessed social unrest, slave uprisings, and struggles among army commanders for control of the state, the fact remains that Roman economic production was relatively high, that Roman victories resulted in the seizure of hoards of wealth, and that large amounts of surplus were being devoted to the arts. One should remember that Augustus succeeded in establishing peace and order, that he spent vast sums embellishing his capital, and that Greek influence stimulated rather than choked off artistic activity.

The last decades of the Republic and the first of the Principate have been justly called the golden age of Latin literature. It was at this time that Cicero (106–43 B.C.) delivered his powerful orations and composed his delightful essays; that Caesar (100–44 B.C.) wrote his *Gallic Wars*; that Vergil (70–19 B.C.) produced Rome's greatest epic poem, *The Aeneid*; that the poets Horace (65–8 B.C.) and Ovid (43 B.C.–A.D. 18) flourished; and that the historian Livy (59 B.C.–A.D. 17) explained how Rome created her vast empire. It was also the period in which the encyclopaedist Varro (116–27 B.C.) summed up Roman knowledge on many subjects; that Catullus (85–54 B.C.) wrote passionately of love in Alexandrian verse; and that Sallust (86–34 B.C.) produced his histories of Catiline's conspiracy and other contemporary episodes. For the most part these works were fresher and more vigorous than contemporary Greek literature. Latin materials were cast in Greek moulds, but the final product had a made-in-Italy stamp on it.

In the other arts Roman achievements of this period were not up to the level of literature. Many Romans who could afford art had acquired their wealth suddenly and were unfamiliar with standards of quality. They did not hold artists in high esteem, nor did they distinguish between the major arts and the minor skills. In general, their tastes ran to works of ostentation and self-glorification, although their constant demand for more artistic surroundings increased and probably reached a high point of quality in the first century B.C. In architecture, where Rome showed the most originality, attention was given to better building materials, city planning, and new forms. Caesar is said to have found Rome a jumbled mass of buildings made from sun-dried brick, but Augustus boasted that he left it a city of marble. The use of concrete faced with brick and the arch resting on piers or columns allowed the construction of new types of structures. The ambitions of Caesar, Pompey, and Augustus led to the beautifying of the old Forum and the construction of new ones, majestic in their proportions. In sculpture there was evidence of greater technical competence and of a desire for a faithful rendering of real objects. The historical relief and portraits, particularly those of Augustus, attained a degree of expression and likeness that were never equalled unless perhaps in the reign of Vespasian (A.D. 69–79) and Trajan (A.D. 98–117). In painting, the selection of the peak of achievement is difficult to determine because of the paucity of remains, yet it would seem from the available evidence that this period marked a high point in technical performance and in freshness of treatment. The murals of the Villa of the Mysteries at Pompeii and of the villa at Boscoreale display concern for theme, composition, and detailed execution which is usually associated with the learned art of the Italian Renaissance.

Although Rome never produced a first-rate original philosopher or scientist, Romans gave attention in the first century B.C. to philosophies and scientific ideas acquired from the Greeks. Stoicism appealed to them because of its stern moral system and emphasis on self-discipline. It fitted in with the need for an orderly world, even if it hurt the lower classes. Epicureanism was even more popular because of its emphasis on material things. It was given brilliant statement by Lucretius (96–55 B.C.) in his

On the Nature of Things. Neo-Pythagoreanism also enjoyed a vogue, for its contention that the human mind had fallen from a state of purity, that it lived in an evil world, and that it could be saved for an eternal life helped to explain obvious conditions and to hold out hope for the future. Yet Stoicism, Epicureanism, and Neo-Pythagoreanism instead of stimulating further exploration led to dogmatic positions.

In general the Romans were not interested in observing, classifying, and ordering data and were even less concerned with attempts to arrive at general statements regarding the physical world that would conform with observed information. If practical results could be obtained by trial-and-error methods or by rules of thumb, Romans did not fret about principles. Most of their science the Romans had derived from Greek or Hellenistic sources, and during the Roman Period most scientific advances were achieved not at Rome but in areas under the direct influence of Greece, particularly in Alexandria. It was from this centre that a large portion of the science of the ancient world was passed on, notably to Arabic scholars and from them to Western Europe.

The chief contributions Rome made to science and Rome's greatest interest in science date from the end of the period under discussion. Instruction in medicine was given in Roman schools towards the close of the Republic, and the most famous medical treatise of Roman times, that by Celsus, appeared shortly after the birth of Christ. The leading Latin work on architecture and mechanics, written by Vitruvius about A.D. 1, indicated that the writer had practical knowledge of windmills, cranes, water-wheels, and, most important of all, a solution to the problem of the transmission of power by gears—an important element in the development of the machine. Furthermore, Romans picked up information about military machines—catapults, battering-rams, and slings—which was put to practical use. They introduced soap, probably from Gaul, and most significant of all, they abandoned the traditional calendar of 354 days, with its extra month every second year, and put into operation on January 1, 45 B.C., the solar calendar of 365 days.[16]

The first two centuries A.D.

With the death of Augustus Rome's most brilliant period of civilisation came to a close. There then followed two centuries in which Rome continued to enjoy imperial power and wealth and to realize important achievements in the arts. Yet in this period weaknesses in Rome's economic and political system became accentuated, and signs of decline in artistic and intellectual activity became apparent, particularly in the second hundred years. Population increases[17] seem to have outstripped growth in the supply of goods; control over human behaviour deteriorated; no new important conquests were made;[18] natural resources were wastefully exploited; and Roman productive and distributive techniques were diffused to other areas. Rome's relative position was weakened as Roman economic and military techniques were adopted by others and as the exchange of goods between the Italian peninsula and the Empire declined.

The chief characteristics of Rome's economic system in this period may be illustrated from the field of agriculture. At this time Rome did not discover any new and important crops or domestic animals, nor did it develop any methods of field or animal husbandry by which to increase production. What it did was to practise known arts of agriculture and to diffuse them more widely. We have already noted that large landholders in Italy began towards the end of the Republic to turn from grain to the olive and the grape. Now we can add that this policy upset the agriculture of places like Greece in which olive and vine cultivation was important, that other areas followed Italy in olive and vine growing, and that Italian wine became so overproduced that the Emperor Domitian (A.D. 81–96) ordered foreign farmers to "plough under" half their vineyards. Grain growing, on the other hand, having declined in Italy and Greece, was expanded in districts like Gaul, where land was being reclaimed from the forest, and in North Africa and on the fringes of Syria, where land had been used exclusively for grazing. In the latter cases, production at first was probably high, but in the long run these semi-arid regions turned into "dust bowls" from which even to the present day they have not recovered, in spite of no appreciable change in rainfall or other climatic conditions. In the course of time, the grain supply of the older and larger cities of Italy became precarious. In the case of Rome, edicts were issued forbidding Egypt to export its grain to other than the capital of the Empire, but such measures depended on power for execution, and when ultimately Rome's power failed, her food supply was in jeopardy.

The diffusion of Roman agricultural methods and crops created in some cases competition between Rome and overseas areas, in others difficulties in supplying the older regions, and in others problems of soil erosion. These issues were, however, no more important than questions of landholding. Because slave labour on large estates became very costly and agricultural management became inefficient, large landowners began to let out their land to tenants (*coloni*) in return for part of their crops and some labour service. The first evidence of such a development appeared on the estates of the Emperors, but it could soon be seen on other holdings, even in the East. The new estates tended to produce more for their own needs than for trade, which militated against the existing division of labour and exchange and thus helped ultimately in destroying the basis of Rome's economic system.

In many respects the history of industry in the first two centuries A.D. was similar to that of agriculture. No important industrial inventions were made and applied; no new techniques which might have revolutionized production were devised; and no radically new products were created. What the Romans did was to pick up industrial techniques and products in the Eastern Mediterranean and to diffuse them in the Western Mediterranean and to the lands north of Italy. This process of diffusion was apparent along trade routes, around camps of Roman soldiers where cities frequently grew up,[19] and at places where the presence of natural resources attracted Roman capital and Roman methods of production. As the process of diffusion went on, Italy turned away from the manufacture of staples and laid more and more emphasis upon luxury goods. Western Mediterranean lands profited most in this development, for they had resources of minerals and of wood superior to those of Italy and the Eastern lands. Hence the industrial phase of military potential increased in the West and declined relatively in the East and in Italy.

In many branches of industrial production the West went through a minor industrial revolution in the first two centuries A.D. Not only was there a great development of mining, in many cases conducted by emperors or their agents, but also of metal industries. Swords, daggers, and armour of Spain became justly famous; iron tools and arms of Gaul attained high positions in quality and quantity; and the swords of Noricum found a large market in Italy. Pottery-making was also greatly extended to the north and west of Italy. Until the end of the first century A.D. pottery from Arretium in Italy had a large export market beyond the Alps, but after that date production of pottery in Gaul and Spain, stimulated by business interests and workers who emigrated from Arretium itself, was so successful that Italian potters were unable to compete with it. In like fashion Roman methods of textile production were introduced into Gaul, which became one of the great cloth-producing provinces of the Empire, exporting its common wares to Italy. Italy and other of the old regions therefore produced relatively more for the luxury and fashion trades.

For the most part staple goods were produced in households or small shops, although in industries that required considerable investment or that had a large market production was frequently on a larger scale. The motive energy used in nearly all undertakings was provided by humans. Although Vitruvius, who wrote Rome's most important work on mechanics about 16 B.C., described an undershot water-wheel with gears for the transmission of power, little evidence is available to indicate that this apparatus, which was certainly capable of general use, was employed at all widely. Labour was organized into *collegia*, whose primary purpose seems to have been to defend the interests of free workers against employers and to gain prestige for workers in a world whose upper crust looked askance at manual effort. The *collegia* indicated a division of labour, for among cobblers there were distinct societies for those who made different types of footgear, and among makers of cloth there were wool-workers, linen-workers, fullers, and purple-dyers.

With the increased division of labour, with greater area specialization in production, and with an increased population, Rome was more dependent than ever on imports. In fact, many parts of the Empire and particularly Italy could not have existed as they did without a system of multi-lateral trade. Hence Rome had to do everything possible to encourage trade. She extended her network of roads, both main highways and secondary routes, to the farthest corner of her dominions. Indeed not until the nineteenth century did countries outside the Empire, like Germany and Russia, have roads comparable to those in Roman provinces. Carrying by land was, however, expensive and slow. As was mentioned earlier, the horse harness was inefficient; horses were small; and horse-shoes were simple sandals tied on. The ox, for its part, was not practical for long hauls because of its slow pace. Most bulky commerce moved by water, along rivers or upon the seas. Under the early Emperors traffic on the rivers of new provinces—on the Rhine, Danube, and rivers of Gaul and Britain—grew rapidly. River and land traffic tended, however, to converge upon the seas, and goods from the Baltic,

North, Black, and Red Seas and from the Atlantic and Indian Oceans[20] gravitated towards the Mediterranean. Hence Ostia and Puteoli were undoubtedly the most active shipping centres, and large sums were spent in improving and enlarging their facilities and in making shipping safe from pirates and storms.

In many other ways Rome acted to aid commercial intercourse. Standard systems of weights and measures were established, and a unified coinage system was created for the whole Empire. Roman private initiative furnished the commercial world with banking services, maintained far-flung sales organizations, and endeavoured to regularize trade through merchant guilds. Although the Empire was divided into eleven customs districts and a charge was placed on goods moving from one district to another and also on goods entering towns (the *octrois*),[21] tariff rates were low, ranging from 2 to 5 per cent. ad valorem, and they took the place of other taxes. Some special measures were adopted to protect Italian agriculture and industry, but they were few in number and were seldom enforced. Rome's chief concern was in getting ample supplies for Italy from her Empire.

During the first two centuries after the birth of Christ Rome continued to have considerable wealth and to produce important works of art and of the intellect. Yet, as in Roman economic affairs, so in its civilisation, there were signs of weakness. Human relations deteriorated over struggles for the emperorship, with the appearance of such leaders as the insane Caligula and the pyromaniac Nero, and with the substitution of imperial dictatorship for republican institutions. The individual had less reason than earlier to have a sense of civic responsibility or to nourish great personal ambitions. There was less of a stimulus from the Greeks to attain perfection in the arts, and there was less freedom of thought, as is witnessed by the persecution of the Christians. In general, the range of opportunities for alternative decisions was becoming narrowed.

The field of literature illustrates well what was taking place. Upon the heels of writers of the golden age came a group of literary men who were more renowned for industry and form than for content. The rhetorical tragedies of Seneca (4 B.C.–A.D. 65), the tales of Petronius (died A.D. 66), and the poetic satires of Persius (A.D. 34–62) were either trivial or lacked strength and form. The satirists Martial (A.D. 40–104) and Juvenal (A.D. 60–140), the educator and rhetorician Quintilian (died *circa* A.D. 96), Rome's greatest historian, Tacitus (A.D. 55–120), and the brief renaissance of Greek letters led by the historian Plutarch (A.D. 46–120) raised the average of literary production of these centuries high enough so that they have attained the appellation of "silver age."

Yet the "silver age" of Roman literature was definitely inferior to the "golden age," and hardly more can be said for architecture. Although Roman builders made use of new forms like the rotunda, as in the case of Hadrian's Tomb, buildings of the first two centuries A.D. were distinguished primarily for their massiveness, size, and ornamentation. Even extensive construction throughout the Empire during the reigns of Trajan and Hadrian elicited little originality. Most of it, as seen in coliseums, aqueducts, and forums, was patterned on Roman styles. Painting also declined rapidly after the first century A.D., and sculpture, having attained excellence in portraiture and in reliefs picturing historical events, as in the scenes on Trajan's Column, deteriorated in the second century to heroic equestrian statues, vulgar memorials, and meaningless ornamental pieces. In fact, it is generally said that Rome produced no great work of literature or art after Trajan and Tacitus.

Legal scholarship was maintained on a somewhat higher level after the birth of Christ than were the arts, perhaps because the field was newer and was freer from fixed forms. The father of Roman jurisprudence is considered to have been Scaevola (died 82 B.C.). He made an effort to state legal principles and had a great influence, for example, on Cicero, who sought the "true law." With Augustus and the Empire a group of the legal profession was employed as counsellors, teachers, and advisers to judges with the result that more attention was given to legal scholarship. Gaius (died about A.D. 180) wrote a model for many legal textbooks; Julianus, a contemporary, prepared a digest of law; Paulus (died A.D. 222) wrote on legal theory, identifying law with the equitable and good; and Ulpian (died A.D. 228) produced commentaries on laws and treatises on the functions of magistrates, which provided nearly a third of the Justinian Code.

During the first two centuries A.D. Rome accomplished no more in the field of science than in the century prior to the birth of Christ. The most important scientific work by a Roman in this period was Pliny the Elder's (A.D. 23–79) *Natural History*. It was a compilation of what Rome knew or thought of the physical world and was void of any serious attempt at establishing the sequential relationship of observed data. On the other hand, scholars of the East, who were in contact with Rome, strove to find out the ways in which man and the world functioned. For example, Strabo (63 B.C.–A.D. 21), a native of Pontus, travelled far and wide to collect geographical information, described the formation of alluvial deposits, and explained changes in the earth's crust. Ptolemy (flourished A.D. 150–170) of Alexandria provided the basis for trigonometry, gave π the value of 3·1416, contributed substantially to geographical information, and in the *Almagest* summarized ancient knowledge of mathematics and astronomy—a body of knowledge which went on to Arabic and Western scholars and was adhered to until modern times. Aretaeus (flourished A.D. 130–190), a Capadocian, was the first to describe diabetes and diphtheria. And Galen of Pergamum (A.D. 130–200), the greatest of ancient physicians, extended man's knowledge of anatomy and physiology and presented the first coherent theory of the inter-action between external environment and the human organism—an achievement that ranks in the forefront of Greek scientific thought.

In philosophy, the Romans were far from original, again borrowing heavily from Greece. Of all Greek philosophies, Stoicism, as taught by Seneca, Epictetus, and the Emperor Marcus Aurelius, was in vogue primarily in the second century A.D. Its main precepts were that an all-wise Providence controlled the universe by means of natural laws and that man could live according to design of Providence by faithful observance of these laws. Of this philosophy Rome made good use, justifying peace and justice by force. For a time Stoicism was rivalled by Neo-Pythagoreanism, but both ultimately gave way to Neo-Platonism, whose chief exponent was Plotinus (A.D. 205–270), which held that highest knowledge is not attainable by human reason.

The economic decline of Roman Italy from the third to the fifth century A.D.

Within the economy of the Empire at the end of the second century A.D. there were many elements of softness, as we have seen. The greatest of these weaknesses was that Rome relied upon products obtained from the various provinces of the Empire for which goods of equivalent value were *not* given in return. The provinces were to a large extent sustaining Italy, and those north and west of the Alps, at least, were increasing their economic potential, while Italy's productive capacity was relatively withering away. How long Italy could continue to be supported by others in the manner to which it had become accustomed depended largely upon the degree to which she could satisfy the provinces by providing them with protection, peace, and economic progress and to the extent also to which she could bend them to her will by force.

The manifestations of this basic problem were many. Wealthy Romans failed to re-invest much of their capital in productive enterprise but, on the contrary, used a large portion of it for luxuries—for show places, circuses, and worse. Similarly they had little understanding of, or concern for, the lower classes, except to keep them quiet. The fact that they lived off others far removed from them made them callous to the effects of ruthless exploitation of resources or to the importance of technological advance. They "cropped" mines in wasteful fashion; they "mined" land, especially destroying grassland and forests in semi-arid regions; they worked labour to exhaustion, discouragement, and apathy; they actually prohibited the introduction of new techniques; and they failed to maintain drainage and irrigation works where they were absolutely essential.[22]

After the second century A.D. Rome did not conquer any new and wealthy areas which could be despoiled of accumulated riches. In the absence of booty and with increased governmental expenses the state had to rely more exclusively than formerly upon the proceeds of current taxation both at home and abroad. Tax rates were increased; tax rolls were periodically revised and tightened; and new taxes, even on land in Italy, were introduced under Diocletian (284–304). With higher taxes and no greater, and in some cases declining, production, the tax burden weighed heavily on people. A point was ultimately reached, as it usually is, where the consequences of tax evasion seemed less onerous than tax-paying. One of the groups particularly hard-hit by heavy taxes was that of the large landholders. Their assets were visible, which made tax evasion difficult; and furthermore, if they were members of municipal senates, as they often were, they were personally liable for the collection of taxes. Consequently many owners of large estates gave up producing for the market and became more self-sufficient. Sometimes the estate owners formed small armies, established their own judicial system, and had their own prisons. In fact, they declared their independence —a policy which struck at the very vitals of the Roman economic system of exchanging goods.

By heavy taxation Rome hoped to get the wherewithal to cover its expenses, but when this method proved insufficient, the state turned towards inflation (end of second century). This expedient, once begun, was resorted to time and time again in the third century, the value of some coins reaching 2 per cent. of par. One of the results of this policy was that it destroyed the monetary unity of the Empire, cities and provinces issuing their own coins. Rising prices, which accompanied devaluation, meant that state officials, soldiers, and all others on more or less fixed salaries saw their real wages go down. Businessmen in the cities cried out against uncertainties created by debasement, lamenting the fact that loans made in coins of a given metallic content were repaid in coins worth a fraction as much. Even the *coloni* suffered, for most of their surplus went to lords, and goods in commerce which they needed were priced beyond their reach.

The trend towards declining production, heavy taxation, debasement of the coinage, and growing economic independence of the large estates was accentuated by a disorganization of the social and political structure by which relations among men were regulated. As the amount of goods available to the ruling classes fell off, these classes became engaged in a struggle to maintain their former economic status. Thus knights, bureaucrats, and commanders of armies lined up in contest against senatorial and privileged urban groups, while the lower classes threw their lot in with the side that would give them the most or merely resorted to grabbing what was nearest at hand. Clear evidence of this conflict was apparent when the Praetorian Guard put the emperorship up for auction. Shortly afterwards, the Emperor Septimius Severus (193–211), a former commander of armies in the provinces, frankly adopted a policy of taxing or confiscating the property of senators and urban businessmen in order to pay his soldiers enough to secure their support.

Not long after his death an effort was made to effect peace between the Senate and the armies, but emperors did not have sufficient authority to achieve their ends. From 235 to 285 only two of twenty-six emperors died a natural death, and at one time there were thirty claimants to the throne. Nor did the central government have enough power to maintain civil peace. Poverty-stricken landholders, bankrupt businessmen, urban workers, *coloni*, slaves, and riotous elements from the armies pillaged far and wide in Gaul, Sicily, Italy, North Africa, and Asia Minor. In 235, a band of brigands made a sweep through Italy. In 238, civil war broke out in North Africa. In 268, *coloni* in Gaul attacked several cities. And in 269, slaves in Sicily revolted.

Taking advantage of this turmoil, barbarians beyond the frontiers of the Empire broke through the cordons drawn against them. Goths went down the Danube and raided Asia Minor. Alamanni drove across the Danube. Franks broke through the Rhine barrier and pillaged as far as Spain (257 and 275). Saxon pirates preyed on the English Channel. Berbers plundered in North Africa. And Sassanians from Iran pushed into the Mesopotamian Valley and in 259 destroyed a Roman army and its emperor commander.

Wars, plagues, poor food supply, and a growing reluctance to raise children resulted in a decline in the population—a reduction estimated to have been for the whole Empire about one-third of the total population during the third century, and probably a larger proportion in Italy. The reduction in population led to enlisting barbarians in the armies, even for higher commands in the early fourth century, to new waves of invaders, and to the settlement of the newcomers within the Empire.

Efforts to bring order out of chaos were not wanting, but they were of little avail until Diocletian came to the throne (284–304). He had been commander in the East and had emerged the victor from a struggle between rival armies. He realized the absolute necessity of having a strong military force to support him and to this end united all Roman armies under his personal command, as Augustus had done much earlier. At the same time he increased the mobility and striking power of the military by using heavily armed cavalry and archers.[23] To enhance his prestige, he added to the practice of emperor worship and introduced a considerable amount of regal and courtly falderal from the East. He created a despotism in which his voice was supreme and that of the Senate a mere murmur. In order to minimize difficulties attending accession to the throne, he associated with himself a second and inferior emperor and two vice-emperors. For the purpose of strengthening his position, he abolished all semblance of local autonomy, and he persecuted dissident groups, particularly Christians. To increase production, he attempted to establish a "controlled economy" by regulating the *collegia*, supervising the large estates, and fixing prices.[24] Finally he revised the tax system in order to get more revenue, and he reformed the coinage in an effort to provide a stable currency.

With all these changes, however, Diocletian failed to reconcile rival groups of the population or notably to arrest the forces at work destroying Rome's economy. His system of two emperors and two vice-emperors merely created rivals to the throne. His economic controls proved unpopular and unworkable. In short, his entire programme did little to stem Rome's disintegration. All this became painfully apparent during the reign of Constantine (306–337) who succeeded him. This Emperor, although he was converted to Christianity and removed one sore spot in Rome's ailing anatomy by stopping persecution of his coreligionists, was unsuccessful in realizing Diocletian's concepts for the restoration of Rome. The military returned again to the status of rival cliques; the frontiers were guarded by a few peasant soldiers; and the capital was removed from Rome to Byzantium, renamed Constantinople, which was a preliminary step to the division of the Empire into West and East.

In the last half of the fourth and during the fifth century the forces that were gnawing out the vitals of the Roman Empire took their most ferocious bites. The growing economic independence of local units, the breakdown of trade, and internal disorders continued their devastating work. Perhaps, however, the most voracious of all were the "barbarians." On all the frontiers pressures were increasing which the Romans could not control. Persians invaded Mesopotamia and Armenia; the Berbers ravaged North Africa; and the West Goths, pressed at their rear by Huns from Central Asia, were allowed to cross the Danube and settle in Roman territory. But almost immediately they turned on the Emperor of the East and by defeating him in the crucial Battle of Adrianople (378) gave the signal for a general rush of barbarians into the Empire. Some of these people infiltrated, finding employment as soldiers and even commanders of Roman armies. Leaders of this type not only learned military techniques from the Romans but had the advantage of numerous fifth columnists. Thus the so-called "barbarian invasions" were not just stampedes of wild human hordes that tore the Romans to bits. They were the coming of people who were familiar with Roman methods of warfare, were led by commanders often with Roman experience, and were equipped and supported by the products of industry established on Roman patterns. Thus Rome's diffusion of her techniques worked against her in the final showdown. To say that Rome fell is somewhat misleading. She wasted away.

The onslaught of the barbarians upon the Empire had a dramatic climax in spite of the fact that Rome was only a rotten shell. The West Goths invaded Italy, sacked Rome in 410, and finally wound up in Gaul and Spain. Vandals from eastern Germany plunged through Gaul and Spain to North Africa, whence they despoiled Rome in 455. The Huns preyed on the Eastern Empire, raided Gaul and Italy (451–452), and finally disappeared in Eastern Europe. The East Goths invaded Italy (489–493), established their chief as emperor, and were absorbed in the population. Jutes, Angles, and Saxons from north-eastern

Germany invaded Britain; Burgundians came into south-eastern Gaul; and Franks moved into Gaul.

In the Eastern Empire there was also an infiltration of barbarians, but there the newcomers, when they attained the emperorship, were able to maintain their authority, the dignity of their office, and their frontiers. It was, indeed, the Eastern Empire, which lasted until 1453, that kept alive much of Eastern Greco-Roman culture during the Middle Ages. One of the early Eastern emperors, Justinian (527 to 565) succeeded in reuniting Italy to the Empire, but after his death invading Lombards from northern Germany undid his work, and Italy became a series of independent states. In this condition the Mediterranean world moved into the Middle Ages.

As the political and economic structure of the Roman Empire fell apart from the third to the sixth century A.D., Roman art and learning went to pieces with it. Literary men devoted their energies to copying, compiling, and commenting upon the works of classical authors. Philosophical writing was reduced to weaving aphorisms and moral maxims for schoolboys. Historical composition degenerated to the simplification of earlier writers and to anecdotal biographies. Scientific treatises were collections of fables and the reiteration of earlier second-rate writings. Legal scholarship declined sharply after the absolutism of Diocletian, and the law itself lost its vitality. The Justinian Code, prepared in the sixth century, summed up Roman legal developments and was a sort of last testament of Roman legal accomplishment. Painting, sculpture, and architecture became less original and more crude, artists failing to create new and vigorous forms of expression. Learning became more stereotyped, being restricted to the seven "liberal arts"—grammar, rhetoric, and dialectic (the *trivium*) and arithmetic, music, geometry, and astronomy (the *quadrivium*).

What creative activity there was in the three centuries being considered came more and more to be associated with Christianity. This religion, which had many of the characteristics of other Eastern cults, preached that one should treat one's neighbour as oneself and that salvation after death was the reward of a good life. Such doctrines had a particular appeal, especially to the lower classes, in a politically, economically, and socially disorganized society. Christianity, unlike any other cult, except its parent Judaism, taught that there was only one God and that its members should not bow down before Roman gods. Such an attitude was difficult for Romans to condone, because in spite of their traditional tolerance in religious matters, they believed that their welfare depended upon the extent to which they pleased their own deities. Yet Christianity spread in spite of persecution because of the relevance of its teaching to existing conditions, the ardour of its missionaries, and the diffusion of its doctrines through the dispersion (*diaspora*) of the Jews.

As Christianity grew in extent and popularity throughout the Empire, it developed a church organization for the government of its affairs. Before the weakening authority of the secular state, the Church assumed a position at least equal to that of the state, for it regarded all human institutions to have been created by God and hence limited by His will and His vicars on earth. Church and state were to share in governing men's lives, but the separation of jurisdiction was not made precise—a situation that gave rise to a lasting conflict in Western culture.

Christianity was, however, more than a political force—it came to dominate men's lives and to furnish inspiration for all their creative activity. In the realm of philosophy the Church Fathers endeavoured to find answers to the fundamental questions raised by classical philosophers. Their answers were as complete as they were simple. God was the ultimate reality; He revealed *truth*; and *His* will explained human history. These precepts necessitated proof of the existence of God, reconciliation of them with observed phenomena, and defence against heretics and persecutors. To these ends such early Church scholars as Origen (185–254), whose efforts centred on exegesis of the Scriptures and the preparation of a systematic Christian theology; Jerome (340–420), whose translation of the Bible, known as the Vulgate, became the accepted version; and Augustine (354–430), whose *The City of God* is generally considered as the most important Christian book after the Bible, worked with skill.

The most important product of Christian literature was the *New Testament*, written mostly in the second half of the first century A.D. But there were also sermons, Christian epics, romantic tales about saints, liturgy, and hymns which had merit. Christianity also provided inspiration for creative activity in the arts, for here was a medium of expression for the propagation of the faith and the glorification of God. Inasmuch as early Christians were from the lower classes, the first Christian art was restricted largely to craftsmanship. With the conversion of wealthier groups after Constantine's adherence to the faith, Christian influence was found in mosaics, which were replacing painting, in sculpture, and in architecture. Many of the products of this inspiration lacked technical perfection and beauty, for these were secondary considerations for Christians. Yet Saint Sophia in Constantinople, constructed by the Emperor Justinian in the sixth century, was one of the masterpieces of Greek Orthodox Christian architecture, and several churches built at Ravenna in the fifth and sixth centuries and adorned with mosaics had charm.

The most lasting and most important influence of Christianity was its ethical and social precepts. It preached the sacredness of human life to a world that had come to have scant regard for individuals of any class. It taught moral responsibility and personal freedom in an age that was woefully in need of both. It proclaimed the virtues of the family and the saintly ideal of abnegation. Although in practice many compromises had to be made between its doctrines and the real world, Christianity provided standards of human conduct of a high social order. Hence Roman civilisation in its decline produced a religion that was to play an important role in Western civilisation for centuries to come.

FOOTNOTES TO CHAPTER V

1 Rome's impact on the aspirations, institutions, and technology of Eastern Europe was not great. Here certain Hellenistic traditions were kept alive during the Middle Ages at Byzantium, whence they were diffused to the eastern Balkans and Russia.

2 The question of Roman citizenship was a complicated one. At first citizenship was a hereditary right of the free-born residents of the city. As Rome expanded she attached some cities to herself and gave its free-born full participation in the Roman Popular Assembly, but, of course, these citizens had to be present in Rome to exercise their privilege. In some cases conquered people were given half-citizenship or probationary citizenship. Full citizenship to all free-born in Italy was not granted until after the Civil War of 90–88 B.C. Citizenship was later extended to free-born outside the peninsula after a given number of years of military service. Only in A.D. 212 were all free-born citizens of cities given Roman citizenship.

3 The population was divided into five classes for voting purposes, with each class having one vote. This system limited further the power of the *plebs*.

4 Early Roman law also established the idea that equity is superior to written law, that arbitrary decisions of judges must be minimized, and that the accepted customs of states, *jus gentium*, must be respected.

5 These were the First Punic War, 264–241 B.C., the Second Punic War, 220–201 B.C., and the Third Punic War, 149–146 B.C.

6 Carthage had amassed a considerable economic surplus. The city itself is estimated to have had a population of about 750,000 at the time of the First Punic War and to have been one of the largest cities, if not the largest, in the Mediterranean world. In spite of considerable economic success, Carthage did not display much creative ability of an intellectual or artistic character. In its culture, as in that of the Phoenician, the "making of money" seems to have been the goal for which men strove. Archaeological remains seem to indicate that the most creative period in Carthaginian art was in the fourth and third centuries B.C., which was also the period, or just after the period, of greatest economic success. See S. Gsell, *Histoire ancienne de l'Afrique du Nord*, Paris, 1913 *ff*.

7 Estimates of Roman population are not accurate. For the Augustan Age at the end of the first century B.C. they vary from 650,000 to 1,200,000. The maximum population during the first century A.D. is placed at 1,600,000.

Before the Second Punic War there were 270,000 male Roman citizens of military age. In 209 B.C. there were about 137,000, but in 163 B.C. there were 337,000 and in 130 B.C., 317,000.

8 Laws limiting the amount of public land that any one person might hold were not enforced.

9 The great Roman works on agriculture, those by Cato, Varro, Vergil, and Columella, were concerned mainly with farming on medium and large estates. A medium estate comprised roughly 150 acres in olives and 60 acres in vines, with other land given over to pasture and some grain. Incidentally, Greek influence on Roman agricultural methods was very great.

10 This practice was begun with the grain laws of Gaius Gracchus in 123 B.C.

11 The payment for imports by coins or by gold and silver bullion was extensive enough to be prohibited by law. For example, Cicero, during his consulship, instructed customs officials at Puteoli to seize gold and silver marked for shipment from Italy (about 63 B.C.).

12 Laws of 217, 104, and 89 B.C. stipulated the weight and purity of Roman coins.

13 After the conquests and re-organization of parts of Asia Minor, Syria, and Palestine by Pompey, 66–62 B.C., the income of the Roman treasury more than doubled, and the publicans were particularly active. In 62 B.C. the interest rate for legitimate transactions in Rome was 6 per cent. Six years later, during Caesar's conquest of Gaul, money in Rome was scarce, and interest rates were at the legal maximum or above.

14 The army was re-organized so that the main force was composed of citizens of Italy. Foreign provincials were usually attached to these forces. Men were shifted around periodically to prevent the creation of an organization hostile to Rome. Augustus established a Praetorian Guard for his protection. He also created a small standing navy.

15 Unfortunately they also introduced the orgies of the cult of Dionysius, or Bacchus, which had such enthusiastic devotees that the Senate took restraining measures (186 B.C.).

16 Every four years a day was added. At about this time the seven-day week was adopted by Caesar, and its use spread rapidly in the Mediterranean world. Earlier the Romans had worked seven days and had gone to market on the eighth. The Greeks divided the month into three ten-day periods.

17 During the second century A.D. the population of Rome is thought to have been between 1,200,000 and 1,600,000 at its highest point and the population of Italy to have been about 14,000,000.

18 In these two centuries the Empire was increased by the acquisition of the greater part of Britain, by land between the Rhine and the Danube, by Dacia, which was north of the lower Danube, by part of Armenia, Assyria, Mesopotamia, and a portion of Arabia.

19 Such cities as Strasburg, Cologne, Mainz, Vienna, Belgrade, and Budapest were built on the sites of Roman camps.

20 Discovery of the action of the monsoons of the Indian Ocean made possible by the first century A.D. a round trip to India in one year. Trajan (emperor A.D. 98–117) connected the Nile and Red Sea, but the extent to which this canal was used is disputed.

21 The Customs Districts were Italy, Sicily, Spain, Britain, Illyricum, Syria, Egypt, North Africa, Bithynia-Pontus-Paphlagonia, and the provinces of Asia.

22 The theory has been advanced that agricultural production declined because of a fall in the fertility of the soil. This theory has some foundation in fact in disafforested and dust-bowl areas. Yet in Egypt, where the Nile floods bring alluvial soil to the land and where fertility is thereby maintained, agricultural production declined in the later Empire.

23 This practice was learned from Sassanian armies. It had been tried by the Romans as early as 260 but was greatly extended by Diocletian.

24 The famous "law of the maximum" was issued in 301. This attempt at price control was unsuccessful.

FOR FURTHER READING

Cyril Bailey (ed.), *The Legacy of Rome* (1924)

J. Carcopino, *Daily Life in Ancient Rome at the Height of the Empire* (1940)

Max Cary, *A History of Rome down to the Reign of Constantine* (1935)

J. Wight Duff, *A Literary History of Rome* (1936)

H. F. Jolowicz, *Historical Introduction to the Study of Roman Law* (1932)

M. Rostovtzeff, *A History of the Ancient World*, Vol. II (1928)

——— *The Social and Economic History of the Roman Empire* (1926)

E. Strong, *Art in Ancient Rome* (1928), 2 Vols.

R. Syme, *The Roman Revolution* (1939)

Tenney Frank, *An Economic History of Rome* (1927)

——— (ed.), *An Economic Survey of Ancient Rome* (1933–1940), 5 Vols.

B. L. Ullman, *Ancient Writing and Its Influence* (1932)

E. L. White, *Why Rome Fell* (1927)

VI

WESTERN CULTURE

WESTERN culture, so-called because it developed primarily in Western Europe, has been the most illustrious successor to Hellenic and Roman cultures and, according to the yardstick of civilisation being employed here, has had one of the greatest civilisations of all time. It has achieved the most extensive and intensive control over physical environment that the world has ever seen. It has attained the greatest supply of goods and services in proportion to population for a longer period of time than any other culture. It has reduced to the lowest minimum the scourges of disease and other natural phenomena. It has produced greater social equality and absence of arbitrary government than any of the cultures treated heretofore in this study. It has created many of the world's most universally and generally recognized masterpieces in architecture, sculpture, painting, literature, and music. And it has practised one of the highest systems of intellectual activity, that of science, or the ordering in a sequential fashion of knowledge about the physical and social world.

Its greatest weakness, and weaknesses it does have, has been its inability to curtail strife, particularly among its various political segments. It has not been consolidated politically in a way to prevent internal warfare, a fact that might conceivably be its undoing. What a commentary it will be upon its economic success, its aesthetic accomplishments, and its science, if its powers are dissipated in the destruction of what it has created !

A synopsis

Of all the attainments of Western culture, none is more remarkable or more fundamental to an understanding of other achievements than the economic. In no other society has such a large population enjoyed equivalent well-being. The basic explanation of its material superiority is to be found in advances in technology, greater utilization of natural resources, a more extensive division of labour, greater investment in enterprise, a more efficient organization of economic activity, and an accepted view that material betterment is highly desirable. Among technological changes, the use of the machine driven by non-human energy stands out as the most significant. Indeed, man's control over physical things has been revolutionized and multiplied by the machine—a mechanical contrivance capable of producing goods many times more abundantly per unit of human input than any other method. In time the machine came to be made of, and to be driven by, inorganic materials. Thus the stored-up wealth of nature began to be tapped, and such stores provided more material and energy than were obtainable solely from organic sources. Yet, as this development took place, the supply of organic products, particularly foodstuffs, was increased, which permitted the maintenance of larger populations.

Western Europe and the Western Hemisphere, the second great centre of Western culture, were richly endowed by nature with those resources, especially fertile land, coal, and iron, which were to play such an important role in economic activity. Improved methods of transportation, however, made it possible for Western culture to draw upon the natural resources of the entire inhabited world. These means of transportation account for Western culture's having removed India, China, and Siberia from their isolation and for having obtained from these and other areas both techniques and goods. Finally, improved methods of communication, particularly movable type and power-driven printing presses, allowed Western Europe easily to exchange new ideas.

Then, too, Western culture has had a remarkable organization of economic activity. A highly developed money economy has made possible an extreme division of labour. In fact, those districts within Western society that have the highest output of goods and services per capita are precisely those where the division of labour and material resources per operative are the highest. Furthermore, institutions, including the crucial one of interest-taking, have grown up to effect a concentration of capital which has made possible the development of large enterprises and the exploitation of ever greater resources. There has also been a distribution of wealth such that, compared with other cultures, the masses have greatly improved their lot. Indeed, they have had such a large share of purchasing power that investment in the production of goods has been encouraged. The wage system—the dependence of workers on a wage for obtaining the necessities of life—has made men work; and the profit system— a desire of investors for gain—has stimulated efficiency in the organization of the economy for the production of goods and services. In general, Western culture has enjoyed great economic expansion in spite of ups and downs; and economies always function best where there is growth.

These economic characteristics of Western culture were not always thus. They developed to the point described through many centuries and many vicissitudes. Even a general account of this history is difficult to grasp, and consequently a brief statement of its major aspects will assist the reader in understanding what is to follow. For this synopsis, we must return to the end of the Roman Empire when Western European economy was decidedly retrogressive.

At the beginning of the Middle Ages there was comparatively

little trade between distant places; industrial production had fallen drastically; and agricultural output was primarily for local consumption. To make matters worse, the Mohammedan conquest of a large part of the Mediterranean at the beginning of the eighth century and the antagonism of Christian Europe to this rival religion brought trade between the Mediterranean and Western Europe almost to a standstill.

During these centuries, however, Venice and certain of the southern Italian towns maintained commercial relations with Constantinople and the Eastern Mediterranean and did not suffer the same economic eclipse as their neighbours to the north. Then, by the eleventh century, trade in the Mediterranean revived, and this brought a new prosperity to the north Italian cities and to the French and Spanish towns of the Mediterranean coast. In the meantime, that is, from the ninth to the eleventh century, commerce between distant places developed in the North Sea and Baltic area. By the latter date the two main trading districts, that in the north and that in the Mediterranean, had made contact and were exchanging their various products. In both these centres and along the routes between them, the use of money became more extensive; towns grew and became more active; and industry for distant markets took a new lease on life. These changes brought with them greater economic surplus, which was used both for investment and for aesthetic and intellectual activity. There was a continued development of economic life, and in the twelfth century there was a revival of learning and the arts known as the Twelfth-century Renaissance.

The course of economic progress appears to have been broken with the opening of the fourteenth century. Famines, the Black Death, failures among Italian businessmen, the Hundred Years' War from the middle of the fourteenth century to the middle of the fifteenth century, and social disturbances raised havoc with economic activity. Far-reaching as these disasters were, however, they failed to push Western Europe into another dark age.

They retarded but did not destroy the new economy. Recovery was certain by the latter half of the fifteenth century, with the Low Countries, France, and Italy leading the way.

At the beginning of modern times, *circa* 1500, the discovery of routes to India and the New World proved an enormous boon to Portugal and Spain, to England, and to the Low Countries. But the countries in the Iberian peninsula soon lost their advantages, and their economies, based on a monopoly of trade with the New World and the importation of precious metals, foundered in the seventeenth and eighteenth centuries. Portugal and Spain were accompanied in their decline by Italy, which was situated off the new trade routes, and by the Germanies, which were devastated by civil strife during the Thirty Years' War (1618–1648). The Northern Netherlands, France, England, and Austria were the centres of greatest prosperity in the seventeenth century, and to them may be added the Germanies in the eighteenth century. Precisely in these areas the greatest artistic and scientific advances were made in these two centuries.

Towards the close of the eighteenth century, the accumulation of knowledge about mechanics and metallurgy had reached a point where it was possible to use machines driven by non-human energy to produce goods on a large scale. Similarly in the early nineteenth century knowledge was successfully applied to providing mechanical means for transporting these goods cheaply over vast distances. In a short space of time, it was as though each operative had acquired a thousand slaves to do his bidding, but these were mechanical slaves which could be renewed and augmented almost at will.

The chief advantages of the mechanization of industry and transportation fell initially to England, but Belgium and France soon benefited also. In the last quarter of the nineteenth century, Germany industrialized rapidly, and so too, but to a lesser extent, did Italy, Austria, and Scandinavia. Thus Western Europe became the "workshop of the world," obtaining raw materials and foodstuffs from overseas in exchange for manufactured products and services. From this activity, Western Europe acquired an economic prosperity that probably had never before been equalled. The large supply of goods and services per capita in the countries involved provided a surplus that could sustain a larger population and a more numerous body of scientists, scholars, and artists. Whether or not their work will stand the test of time so that the nineteenth and twentieth centuries will appear to the man of the future as a period of great cultural achievement is difficult to foretell. Perhaps impressionistic painting, the music of Verdi and Wagner, and some architecture will be universally and consistently regarded as of a high order. Of one thing, a degree of certainty can be expressed, that scientific accomplishments have led to a knowledge never before possessed by man and to a control over physical environment never before equalled. Its accomplishments may mark this era as a high point in Western culture.

Whatever the decision of the future may be in this regard, it is clear that the position of Western Europe as the centre of Western civilisation has weakened. Towards the close of the nineteenth century and more definitely as the twentieth century progressed, certain trends began to indicate that Western Europe was losing its economic primacy. Technology became more mobile, spreading rapidly from its place of origin to new areas. Similarly capital for investment became more flexible and sought opportunities for profit on a growing scale outside Western Europe. Thus other areas, notably the Western Hemisphere and particularly the United States, the Far East, Africa, and Russia, began to mechanize their industry and to adopt improved methods of agriculture. Some places with extraordinarily rich natural resources, proximity to large markets, or an efficient labour supply soon learned that they had advantages over Western Europe which they could exploit to their own benefit. Furthermore, antiquated productive equipment, social tensions, political rivalries, and devastating wars hindered progress in the older industrialized regions of Europe.

The fact that Western Europe was not keeping pace economically with the rest of the world was at first not disturbing, for the change was gradual, and Western Europe was receiving large "tribute" in the form of interest on investment from the rest of the world. By the end of World War II, however, after Western Europe had been deprived of so many of its overseas investments to fight the war and had seen such a large part of its property destroyed, its predicament was clear. A large part of the world was taking over the economic ways of the West and in the process was adopting much of Western culture. Economic pre-eminence was passing to regions outside of Europe, particularly to the English-speaking area of North America. As yet these areas have not had time to demonstrate convincingly that they will lead Western culture to new heights. Experience of the past, as recorded in this book, seems to suggest a strong probability that such will eventually come to pass.

The Middle Ages

An analogy has frequently been drawn between the plight of Rome in the fourth and fifth centuries A.D. and that of Western Europe in recent decades. In the two situations there are, indeed, elements of similarity. Both regions experienced a relative decline in productivity and a decline in the rate of population growth. Both suffered from a reduction in the receipt of goods or payments from foreign lands. Both were wracked by war, and both saw the centre of economic primacy move to other places— Rome to Constantinople, and Western Europe to the Western Hemisphere.

Here the obvious similarities cease, for Rome's predicament was much worse than anything Western Europe has so far experienced. The tendency in Rome's case was for the new economy to become overwhelmingly agricultural, with production conducted to meet local needs. Labour became bound to the soil, and, in most parts of the old Western Roman Empire, it was also bound to over-lords by pledges of fealty. Industry and trade on a large scale and for a large market also declined, the depth of commercial activity being reached in the ninth century.[1]

Whether the presence of Mohammedans of Arabic culture in the Western Mediterranean or the local self-sufficiency of Western Europe accounts primarily for this condition need not detain us. The fact is that the use of money, the division of labour, and the organization of business for profit, all declined. Land was almost the sole object of economic activity and condition of wealth, while the relatively small feudal estate was the basis for the only effective political organization of the time. From such an economy and from such political units came little economic surplus that could be devoted either to learning, to the arts, or to economic progress.

Western Europe's emergence from this economic morass of the Dark Ages, which may be considered to have extended from the fifth to the tenth century, was slow indeed. But from the ninth to the eleventh century signs of recovery were visible in two widely separated areas, in Italy and its neighbouring waters and in the North Sea and Baltic region. In both districts economic revival was clearly initiated by trade in which piracy played an important role.

Certain Italian towns, notably Venice, Naples, and Bari, showed the first evidence of change. Arabs had never succeeded in dominating either the Aegean or Adriatic Seas and did not cut trade between Italy and Constantinople, nor did all Italian merchants allow their religious scruples to prevent them from making a profit from trade with Arabian infidels. By the end of the ninth century, commercial exchanges were being made between Italy and North Africa or Syria, while enterprising Venetians found profit and perhaps pleasure in capturing female Slavs, hence the word slave, along the Dalmatian coast for

Arabian harems. By the end of the eleventh century, Venice had established trading posts with special privileges in all those commercial centres of Asia and Europe which were under the jurisdiction of the rulers of Constantinople and had almost a monopoly of the carrying trade among them. She also expanded her commercial activities to the mainland, even to the Alps, for the city was completely dependent upon imports for her food and raw material supplies. What was of extreme importance was that she made money profits from her Eastern trade and paid for at least part of her mainland supplies in money. Thus Venice as carrier and trader gave new life to the institution of money, re-established an economy organized for profit, and renewed the use in business of writing and numerical notation.

At approximately the same time that these changes were taking place in northern Italy, commerce, as has already been stated, was beginning in the North Sea and Baltic region. The Northmen of the Scandinavian peninsula took to the sea in order to obtain a livelihood, for their land was mountainous and poor. They became excellent seamen and explored far and wide, even reaching the Western Hemisphere in the eleventh century. For the most part, they operated as pirates rather than as settlers, but from piracy they passed by the ninth century to legitimate trade. Danes and Norwegians operated chiefly in France, the Low Countries, and the British Isles, while Swedes turned their attention more particularly to Russia. The latter established trading posts (*gorods*) and opened up routes which reached Constantinople. Over these arteries of commerce, they sent women to Arab harems, along with amber, furs, and honey. In return they obtained spices, wines, silks, jewellery, and other luxuries. They also used money, if one may judge from Arab and Byzantine coins found in the Baltic area, and they brought back certain Byzantine cultural influences, Russia having obtained Christianity and architectural forms from the East.

Although the future of Baltic–Black Sea commerce was dark

because of the arduous land journey and the difficulties of protecting shipments, other opportunities were open to the North Sea–Baltic trading area, especially commerce with the Mediterranean. Contacts between the two districts were certainly made by the eleventh century and grew thereafter. By that time, however, events were taking place which led to further development in the two main commercial regions. In the northern centre, trade with nearby lands became more intense, and the people began to specialize in manufacturing goods for their neighbours. Flanders, for example, turned to the production of woollen cloths. In the tenth century, this region was supplying Northmen with textiles for their trade and soon began to import wool from England to supplement its own supply. From the beginning of the twelfth century, Flemish cloth was being sold in Novgorod, and Italian markets were obtaining it in exchange for silks and spices. Production of cloth became a *city* industry and was the foundation for the prosperity and growth in Flanders of Ghent, Ypres, Bruges, and in northern France of Lille, Douai, and Arras. Strangely enough, however, the Flemings themselves concentrated on production rather than on trade, leaving the latter activity to Scandinavians, Italians, and members of the Hanse— merchants of a group of North Sea and Baltic cities.

In the Mediterranean perhaps even more important economic progress was being registered. Now in addition to Venice and southern Italian cities, certain ports, notably Genoa and Pisa, became interested in extending their commercial activity. These cities of the west coast were, however, hemmed in by Mohammedan Arabs and resorted to war to break the barriers against them. Inspired by a combination of commercial and religious considerations—both strong incentives—the Genoese and Pisans made headway, getting a foothold in Sicily and then in 1087 capturing an important Mohammedan town in North Africa which rendered them rich booty. Overjoyed at their good fortune, the Pisans devoted some of their plunder to the construction of their famous cathedral, which stands as a symbol of their success against Islam.

Shortly after this event, Mediterranean trade was further stimulated by the Crusades—Christian wars against the Mohammedans for control of the Holy Places. Beginning in 1096 and continuing for at least two centuries, the Crusaders pushed Islam back. Furthermore, one of the Crusades was successfully directed against the Greek Orthodox capital at Constantinople, a move that weakened Constantinople's control of the Eastern Mediterranean. Nor did the Mohammedan Turks, when they extended their sway in this region, interfere seriously with Christian trade, for they reaped much benefit from it. Thus commerce in the Mediterranean was greatly extended, and it contributed to the economic growth of cities in Italy, southern France, and eastern Spain. To be sure, Venice, Genoa, and others were keen business rivals and at times fought for special advantages, but such strife did not invalidate the fact that in the Mediterranean Sea trade over a large area and an extended money economy were taking shape.

As in the North Sea and Baltic regions, so in the Western Mediterranean greater commercial exchange led to manufacturing for new markets, and both trade and industry stimulated the division of labour. The Italian cities, which had served as suppliers and carriers for all the Crusades except the first, saw a fillip given to ship construction, to the production of weapons and tools, and to the processing of foodstuffs. Furthermore, when Crusaders from beyond the Alps returned home, they demanded Eastern luxuries for which they had developed a taste while at the front. To supply the demand thus created, Italians began to produce some of these luxuries at home, as for example silk cloth at Lucca and jewellery at Venice. When these goods were shipped northward, they were paid for in metallurgical wares and in wool cloth, which was dyed and finished by special processes in Italy, especially at Florence. In such ways, commercial ties between the North Sea–Baltic regions and the

Mediterranean were knit more closely, and industry in both places was developed anew.

As in antiquity so now, most commerce moved by water, for it was the cheapest means of transportation for bulky goods. Gradually larger ships were built, even up to 600 tons' burden, and sailing was improved in the thirteenth century by improvements in the rudder that permitted more successful tacking. By the beginning of the fourteenth century, fleets from Venice and Genoa made annual voyages through the Strait of Gibraltar to the markets of Bruges and London. Traffic on inland waterways also increased, and by the twelfth century canals were being constructed, particularly in the Low Countries, to connect rivers.[2] Land transportation was advanced by the opening of new routes, the construction of bridges, and in the tenth century by the construction of a horse collar that would allow the animal to pull without having his air shut off.

In spite of all these changes, the volume or ease of medieval trade should not be exaggerated. Land transportation was slow, roads were poor, and tolls were numerous. Water transportation also had its limitations, and probably the entire fleets of either Venice or Genoa hardly exceeded the tonnage of the largest twentieth-century liner. Yet the growth of trade was sufficient to lead to economic change in the twelfth and thirteenth centuries—change which in the depth of its impact may be compared with the industrial revolution of the nineteenth century.

Of all the new economic developments none was more basic than a more widespread and intensive use of money. In this respect Western European development was running true to historical form, for in all our previous investigations the appearance of a convenient medium of exchange always accompanied increased commercial activity. In this case a coinage system was created by Charlemagne in the early ninth century which was widely used and which exists at the present time wherever the pound sterling is employed. He established the pound (*livre*, *libra*),

which was divided into 20 shillings (*sous*, *soldi*), that in turn
contained 12 pence (*deniers*, *denari*) each. For the most part,
the coinage of money was as usual a prerogative of a political
authority and at that time was in the hands of princes who had
traditionally provided what money was needed on their estates.
This was perhaps an unfortunate situation, for princes debased
their money when they needed funds to pay off their debts irrespective of the consequences their acts would have on others.
By the end of the twelfth century and the beginning of the
thirteenth, there was such anarchy in money that trading cities
like Venice initiated reforms to provide a more stable medium
of exchange. Yet no scheme has ever been devised to prevent
debasement by the issuer, and the fluctuations in the value of
money were to be a perennial problem.

The great number of princes and autonomous cities meant
that there were many different types of coins. Hence the ubiquitous money-changer came again upon the scene. He found his
business profitable, although somewhat disreputable. Nevertheless, he was soon receiving sums for safe-keeping, was effecting
transfers of funds between debtors and creditors, and was making
loans. Merchants, too, engaged in these banking practices, and
in Italy great banking families, like the Bardi and Peruzzi, became
established. As had happened in both Rome and Greece, the
bill of exchange came into use to facilitate the settlement of
business accounts; the letter of credit put in an appearance; and
bottomry loans to reduce risks to shippers began to be issued.
Most important of all perhaps, for it provided a material incentive
for the accumulation and investment of money, was interest-
taking.

Now the Church was opposed to having money lent at
interest, for, prior to the commercial revolution that we are
describing, loans were usually sought when famine was at hand
or by lords for extravagances beyond their means. This meant
that lenders usually exacted high rates from borrowers. All

interest-taking was dubbed usury, that is, a charge for using a loan, but the term was coined when rates were actually usurious. As investments began to be made to render useful economic services, ways were found to circumvent the Church's antipathy towards interest-taking. Money was lent with the expectation of profit, and the long and slow process of overcoming the Church's compunctions got under way.

With the growth of commerce, new types of business organizations were created or old ones revived. Among them were the fairs where merchants from distant points came together to buy and sell. They were opened to all—a freedom that was exceedingly important in facilitating exchange. These institutions began to appear in the eleventh century, and their number increased during the twelfth and thirteenth centuries. The most famous of the fairs and the only ones to attract merchants from all Europe in the twelfth and thirteenth centuries were those of Champagne in France, which lasted the year round. But other places had similar meetings which varied in size with the amount of trade carried on—Stourbridge, near Cambridge, England, Bruges, Ypres, and Lille in Flanders, and then Lyons and Geneva, which in the fourteenth century outstripped Champagne.

In addition to fairs, there were the merchant guilds, which came into being in the eleventh and twelfth centuries. They were, unlike the fairs, restrictive in character, and were designed by their members, the merchants of a given town, to create a local monopoly and to protect their general interests. As a rule, only members of the guild could buy, sell, or manufacture goods in a town, and foreign traders could do business only with them. Guilds sought privileges and rights from local princes, negotiated with guilds in other towns, encroached upon the powers of local government, and established rules aimed at preventing sharp practices. Above the guilds there were the Hanse, associations of guilds or merchants of various towns, or leagues of towns, which began to be formed in the twelfth century for facilitating trade. The most famous of these groups was the Hanseatic League, composed of cities along the Rhine, the North Sea, and the Baltic, but there were also the Hanse of northern France and Flanders, the Merchant Staplers of England for the export of wool, and others. Below the guilds there were various combinations of interests for the conduct of business, especially partnerships, multiple partnerships, and *commenda*, in which there were sleeping partners, those who invested their funds but who took no active part in management.

At almost the same time that expansion of trade was leading to the creation of new forms of business organizations, the growth of industry was having a similar effect in the realm of manufacturing. Craft guilds began to be established, which, like merchant guilds, aimed to secure monopoly for the production of certain articles, to obtain a degree of political authority, and to lay down regulations for the conduct of their business. These bodies indicate a considerable division of labour, for there were guilds for weavers, dyers, fullers, butchers, and bakers—the number of specialists increasing as time went on. If the members of a guild produced for a relatively large market, especially an export market, the master was a businessman rather than a mere artisan. He often used borrowed capital, employed men as wage earners, sold his wares in an impersonal market, and sought to make a profit. The fact that in the middle of the fourteenth century the town of Ghent in present-day Belgium had 4,000 weavers out of a total population of 50,000 indicates that a considerable degree of specialization in production had been realized and that goods were being produced for more than local consumption.

Those who produced for large markets were interested in technological improvements. Thus we find them in the twelfth century using water power for the first time for other purposes than making flour. They employed it for driving fulling mills and grinding bark for tanning leather. In the thirteenth century, they used it for sawing timber; and in the fourteenth, for turning grindstones in metal-work. Furthermore, the twelfth century saw the adoption of windmills for grinding grain, the making of paper in France and Spain, the installation of improved looms, and the reeling of silk by improved machines. In the thirteenth century the wheel rather than the distaff was used in spinning; and gunpowder began to be employed—an explosive which was to revolutionize the art of war, to increase the vulnerability of fortified castles, and thereby to weaken the position of lords. Also the clock escapement was conceived and applied successfully in the following century, while general clock-making provided the foundation for precision work which was so essential to the development of intricate industrial machines.

With the employment of borrowed capital, hiring of labour for wages, production for an unknown, uncertain, and impersonal market, and the desire for profit, the essentials of the capitalist system came into being. Furthermore, mechanical advances and more extensive use of inorganic power were hints, at least, of the direction in which Western European industry was to move. To a very large extent, however, agriculture was immune to changes in commerce and industry. Its technology remained largely unchanged, and its production was for the most part geared to local needs. To be sure, the increase in population which took place in the twelfth century gave rise to a search for new lands that could be brought into cultivation, as, for example, reclamation of swampy areas in Flanders, the Netherlands, and Germany by means of dikes; and it led also to the colonization by Germans of districts to their east and north-east. Furthermore, there was some specialization in the growing of crops, as in the case of silk in Italy, wool in England, and wine in the Bordeaux area.

The chief effects of the new economic developments in rural areas were the more extensive use of money and the beginnings of the breakdown of feudalism. As wealthy businessmen began to indulge in luxuries of one kind and another, nobles realized that they had to have even more extravagant things if they were to retain their social position. The deliveries of goods and services by serfs to lords did not suffice to provide luxuries, for they could not easily be turned into money. When in the twelfth century the prices of luxuries rose abruptly, lords were hard pressed for funds and in their extremity began to free serfs from certain obligations by means of cash settlements or by substituting money payments for dues in goods and services. Furthermore, serfs might seek alternative employment in cities and could obtain their legal freedom by residence there for a year plus one day. Thus an inroad was made in the institution of serfdom in the twelfth and thirteenth centuries, although remnants of it were not completely abolished until the nineteenth century. As so many times in earlier instances, the growth of commerce and of a money economy led directly to greater legal liberty for the individual.

Another important concomitant of economic development from the eleventh to the thirteenth century was the growth of cities. By 1400, Milan, Florence, Venice, and Paris had populations of 100,000 or more, while London had 50,000 inhabitants and many places had 20,000. In general, the newly built parts of cities were close upon an older fortified place, or burg, and were hence called suburbs, or *Neubürge*, or *faubourgs*. The trading citizens of these new districts were known as bourgeois, as distinguished from the leading citizens, or nobles of the burgs. In most places the newly rich sought political power and often obtained it by force. They sponsored legal systems based on evidence, equity, and business considerations; they opposed arbitrary forms of feudal justice and non-commercial phases of Church (canon) law; and they founded schools so that their sons might acquire elements of education necessary for the conduct of business. In cases where they got political power, they levied taxes for city fortifications and other improvements, thus restoring the public character of taxation; they lent money to city governments; and they sometimes took over the collection of city revenues in return for loans, a practice that gave rise to at least one famous bank, the Bank of St. George in Genoa.

Such evidence as exists shows clearly a considerable economic development in Western Europe from at least the eleventh to the thirteenth century. It was, moreover, a kind of development which permitted the accumulation of surplus that could be used to support cultural and intellectual activity. It was, indeed, accompanied by a definite revival in the arts and learning, the so-called twelfth-century renaissance, as we shall see in more detail later.

Economic advance did not, however, go forward entirely unimpeded. Bad harvests and wars periodically resulted in arresting commerce and industry, and then in the fourteenth and early fifteenth centuries a concatenation of events led to a general economic setback. Perhaps Western Europe had reached the limits of its technology, resources, and business institutions, but in any case economic activity appeared to have reached a plateau by the first decades after 1300. Then a series of misfortunes began. From 1315 to 1317 a great famine ravaged all Europe—the worst European famine to that date of which we have any record. This catastrophe was followed by the Black Death, which from 1347 to 1350 is believed to have carried off a third of the population of Western Europe, to say nothing of those who perished before and after those years. The calamitous character of these events was reflected in the bankruptcies of several of the leading bankers of Italy, the beginning of the decline of the Champagne fairs, civil strife in Italy, political anarchy in the Germanies, and the Hundred Years' War (1337–1453) which ruined France and exhausted England. A shortage of labour led serfs to demand and get the abolition or commutation into money payments of more of their obligations to lords; craftsmen to seek a voice in government; and journeymen—the wage earners—to agitate against guild masters.

Disastrous as these events were, the destruction should not be exaggerated. Europe was not laid waste—it was only retarded in its development. In Italy, for example, commercial relations with the Levant were maintained, and Eastern goods continued to be sent to the north through Alpine passes or via Gibraltar, even though in reduced quantities. In the Low Countries, too, production never ceased altogether, and conditions were such that individuals could continue to amass fortunes. Moreover, recovery in France under stronger royal authorities was relatively rapid, and England not only survived but seems to have developed some industry while cut off from European suppliers. Spain and Portugal also weathered the storm, the latter undertaking explorations for new lands along the African coast and for a new route to India. Only the Germanies continued to suffer seriously because of political unrest, but even here Rhenish cities conducted a profitable commerce, and a printer at Strasbourg is credited with having invented movable type. In the later half of the fifteenth century recovery from the depths of stagnation was fairly general. Indeed this period can be considered as a prosperous one, a time in which new wealth was being accumulated that was to support the artistic and intellectual accomplishments of the Renaissance.

At the very end of the fifteenth century an all-water route to India and the discovery of the New World were to give a new fillip to Europe's recovery. They were to lead to a new expansion of commerce, to a further development of the use of money, and to greater industrial production. These events at the very end of the Middle Ages were to usher in a new era of economic progress —an era that historians designate as the beginning of modern times. This progress was to follow along the lines of economic institutions which had become clear from the eleventh century onward.

Economic development, 1500–1800

From time to time in history a number of factors have combined in such a way as to inaugurate far-reaching changes in the course of human activity. This was the case regarding the discovery of an all-water route to India and the Far East and the finding of the New World. Prior to these momentous events, Europeans had made important improvements in navigation, shipbuilding, and seamanship. They had acquired the compass, which was probably a Chinese invention, by the twelfth century and were using it generally in the fifteenth. They had procured from the Arabs the astrolabe, a forerunner of the quadrant and sextant,[3] which permitted voyagers to determine their position relative to the sun and stars. They had better charts, maps, and astronomical tables. And many of them believed, along with Eratosthenes of ancient Alexandria and contrary to popular belief, that the earth was round and not flat. They had developed more seaworthy ships, like the caravel, and some of their seamen were being trained for long voyages, particularly in a school established by Prince Henry the Navigator of Portugal.

Among other factors which undoubtedly contributed to the making of the great discoveries were a religious zeal created by the "crusades" of the Portuguese and Spaniards against the Moors and current stories about "lost Christian kingdoms," somewhere out in the unknown, which ought to be saved. Then there was a generally awakened interest in discovery, which was combined with love of adventure and sheer curiosity about what was beyond the seas. There was a desire for gain, whetted by the knowledge that Venice had made great profit from Eastern trade and that a new trade route to the East would secure a part of this rich melon.[4] Finally in Western Europe individual feudal princes had amalgamated enough territory under their authority at the expense of other princes to provide both men and equipment for expensive explorations.

Motivated by such considerations, Europeans began early in the fifteenth century to venture forth into the Atlantic. The Madeira Islands were settled about 1420; possession of the Canaries was contested by Spain and Portugal, beginning in 1425;

and the Azores were discovered or re-discovered about 1430. In 1434 an expedition inspired by Prince Henry the Navigator of Portugal rounded Cape Bojador, and about ten years later another group rounded Cape Verde. In 1488 the Portuguese Diaz sailed around the Cape of Good Hope; and four years later the Genoese, Columbus, sailing under Spanish colours, reached the New World. Between 1497 and 1499 Vasco Da Gama, a Portuguese, made the first all-water round trip to India. Thenceforth discoveries and explorations came thick and fast. John and Sebastian Cabot, Genoese sailing for the English in 1498, explored the North American coast from Delaware to Labrador; Amerigo Vespucci, a native of Florence, explored the Brazilian coast for Portugal (1501); Magellan circumnavigated the earth under the Spanish flag (1519–1522); and subsequently followers of these men penetrated into the interiors of the New World and staked out claims for their sovereigns.

The area opened to Europeans by the early discoverers was enormous. It comprised the Persian Gulf, India, China, the Malay Peninsula, the Spice Islands, the coast of Africa, almost all the coast of the Americas, the interior of Mexico, the West Indies, Madagascar, the Philippines, and some of the west coast of South America. Here was an empire which exceeded in size the wildest dreams of the most enthusiastic expansionist.

More important than territorial extent were, however, the economic potentialities of the overseas territories for the economic development of Western Europe. Some of these potentialities were soon visible, for early experience indicated that great profits could be made in trade with the newly discovered places. Da Gama returned from his first voyage with a cargo on which was realized a profit exceeding by sixty times the entire cost of his expedition. Magellan's voyage, although only one of his five ships returned, showed a handsome gain. And early Spanish conquerors brought back fabulous amounts of gold and silver which they obtained from the Indians of Peru and Mexico and which were to contribute mightily to the growth of Europe's money economy. Finally, the alleged wealth of the New World aroused the imagination of Europeans to such a pitch that they began one of the greatest colonizing movements in all history—a movement that can be compared with the migrations of the Peoples of the Sea at the end of the second millennium B.C. or with the barbarian migrations at the end of the Roman Period.

Of all these developments, the growth of trade with distant places had one of the most profound effects upon Europe's economy. In the absence of adequate statistics, it is impossible to give an accurate picture of the growth of European commerce with the rest of the world during the three centuries from 1500 to 1800, but some impression of the increase can be had from scattered data. For example, Portugal is reported to have received 1,300 tons of pepper from the East in 1503, and Portuguese royal profits from Eastern trade are said to have amounted to as much as $1,250,000 (1940 value) per year. Spain imported nearly a thousand million dollars (1932 value) of gold and silver bullion from 1503 to 1660; and English trade in the eighteenth century is thought to have quadrupled. Certainly, the new trade was relatively very great and brought economic advantage to those parts of Europe that were most directly engaged in it. These areas were located on Europe's Atlantic seaboard, and gradually their commerce came to exceed that of Mediterranean cities—a shift that is known as the commercial revolution of the sixteenth century. On the Atlantic coast were to be found, then, districts where economic progress was most pronounced and incidentally where the greatest intellectual and artistic achievements were to be realized. Nevertheless, north Italian and south German cities still had accumulated wealth, retained a considerable amount of trade, and contributed to the intellectual life of the sixteenth century.

Of course, the economic situation of the various European states on the Atlantic seaboard differed profoundly and changed

THE DEVELOPMENT OF TRADE IN EUROPE, LATER MIDDLE AGES

TO INDIA AND CHINA

TO INDIA AND CHINA

TO INDIA

Astrakhan

VOLGA R.

Caspian Sea

TIGRIS R.

Baghdad

EUPHRATES R.

Palestine

Black Sea

DON R.

Constantinople

DNIEPER R.

Kiev

DANUBE R.

Alexandria

Cairo

Mediterranean Sea

Novgorod

Narva

Riga

Danzig

Breslau

Cracow

Vienna

Leipzig

Thorn

Lübeck

Hamburg

Magdeburg

Nuremberg

Augsburg

Venice

Florence

Rome

Naples

Tunis

Stockholm

Bergen

Bremen

Amsterdam

Bruges

London

Southampton

Bristol

Paris

Basel

Bologna

Milan

Genoa

Lyons

Marseille

Bordeaux

Barcelona

Valencia

Toledo

Lisbon

Atlantic Ocean

MILES

0   200   500

fundamentally as time went on. At first Portugal had a complete monopoly of the all-water trade route to the East, and this commerce appears to have provided that country with enough profits to satisfy it or to have absorbed all its available energies. Inasmuch as the Portuguese made no serious attempt to distribute their Eastern wares to the North, that business fell to others and particularly to the Dutch. Before the end of the sixteenth century, these people began to go directly to the East for goods previously obtained from Portugal. This practice not only undermined the very foundations upon which Portuguese prosperity rested, but it also led to the establishment of Dutch colonies in the East from which Dutch merchants radiated in search of trade. From this commerce the Dutch reaped a great harvest and became in the seventeenth century one of the most important mercantile and shipping peoples of Western Europe.

Like Portugal and the northern Netherlands, Spain obtained large benefits from trade, but from trade with the New World rather than with the East. Yet unlike these states, she discovered in her new possessions vast riches of precious metals either in hoards amassed by Indians or remaining in the ground awaiting industrious miners. At first she obtained large supplies of gold and silver through robbing the natives, but as this source was drained dry, she turned to mining such deposits as that at Potosí. Unfortunately for Spain this wealth did not lead to extensive economic development at home. Much of Spanish bullion went abroad in payment for goods needed for domestic consumption or for export to the colonies, but it did permit a relatively small class of beneficiaries to enjoy considerable luxury and to support an artistic movement in the sixteenth and early seventeenth centuries. In the seventeenth century, however, Spain lost its position of economic eminence as others gobbled up much of her colonial trade. The supply of bullion from the New World declined; her government fell into the hands of weaklings; and the fortunes of war turned against her. By the eighteenth century, she had become a second-rate economic and political power.

Britain and France, for their part, did not early acquire territories overseas with which they could have at once a profitable trade or from which they could obtain large quantities of gold and silver. For the most part their colonies were such that production in them had to be developed before they were of much value. By the end of the seventeenth and in the eighteenth century *la mise en valeur* of the colonies was being realized, and the mother-lands were receiving raw materials and foodstuffs in return for exports of manufactured goods. In the same centuries, moreover, these two powers encroached upon Dutch commercial prerogatives in the East and the British, at least, made large inroads into Spain's trade with Latin America. But no sooner had the position of the Dutch been weakened, than the British and French became involved in a long struggle for world empire. In this "Second Hundred Years' War," which came to an end with the close of the Napoleonic Wars (1815), the British had extended their sway to include India, Canada, South Africa, Ceylon, islands in the West Indies, and many smaller possessions. And what was most important, Britain rose to the position of the leading mercantile nation of the world.

As first Portugal and Spain, then the Netherlands, and finally France and Britain vied for first place in the economy of Western culture, economic changes were bringing about the development of modern capitalism. In brief, this system may be described as one in which individuals own capital in the form of land, productive equipment, raw materials, money, or other valuables, who hire labour for wages in an impersonal market, and who with their capital and hired labour strive to produce goods and services on a large scale in the hope of reaping a profit. Although all the components of the definition are essential to the institution itself, all did not have equal roles in the historical process whereby modern capitalism came into being. Perhaps the most crucial component—the one that acted as a catalyst upon the others—

was money, particularly money that could be lent out at interest. Inasmuch as money is a form of capital that has relatively great mobility and that through interest charges can be made to earn a profit without much supervision by the owner, it can be amassed from many small sources until a large amount is obtained and can be put to work with other factors of production to earn a profit. Its use facilitates the creation of large-scale new business ventures, and they lead, in turn, to the establishment of impersonal relationships between employer and employee and between producer and consumer.

Money had been the medium of exchange in many cultures prior to the one that we call Western, but never before had it succeeded in penetrating so deeply and permeating so extensively all economic life. This is a fundamental fact. The reasons for it are many, but two of the more important ones can be mentioned briefly. The first is that the supply of money in relation to the supply of goods and services became very great. The production of gold and silver in Europe increased dramatically in the late fifteenth century and then again in the sixteenth as bullion came in from the New World. One estimate has it that the stock of precious metals in Europe tripled between 1500 and 1650. The second reason is that Western Europe developed a system of credit instruments—bills of exchange, promissory notes, letters of credit, and bank notes—which increased the supply of exchange mediums far beyond anything possible with coins and far beyond anything that had existed previously. Just by way of example, let us cite the case of the Bank of Sweden, which extended its issue of bank notes by over 1,300 per cent. from 1737 to 1762.[5]

Such increases in the supply of money as have been mentioned led to a greater exchange of goods for money and to the establishment of a more extensive price system—two developments that tended to impersonalize relations between employers and employees and between producers and consumers. Furthermore the increased supply of money in the sixteenth and the first half of the seventeenth century led to a rise in price levels which for Spain and Britain are estimated to have been in the neighbourhood of 300 per cent. Subsequently prices reacted downward until the beginning of the eighteenth century, when they went up once again to the period after the Napoleonic Wars. Thus with a money economy and its concomitant price system a new element of fluctuation was introduced into economic life on a larger scale than hitherto. This was significant, for as prices rose, wages failed to keep pace. The result of this situation was that with labour costs of production reduced, profits tended to increase; and this "profit inflation," as it is called, was a buoyant factor in economic development.

Incidentally another aspect of money should be mentioned here. Over long periods of time money has tended to lose value, or to put it in another way, prices in terms of a given medium of exchange have gone upward. The reasons for this phenomenon are complex, but perhaps the most important single explanation of it is that individuals and governments are inclined to spend beyond their ability to meet their obligations and, in order to free themselves from debt, demand and get cheaper money. Furthermore, it is clear that the capitalist system operates more satisfactorily when prices are reacting upward than when they are heading downward, and this fact makes for easy-money policies.

In any case, as modern capitalism developed, it brought into being new methods and organizations for performing its vital services: (1) the issuing of coins by state mints, (2) the issuing of bank notes by banks, (3) the transfer of funds, (4) the accumulating of capital, (5) the investment of capital, (6) the minimizing of certain risks by diversification or insurance. Gradually, states, while retaining their power of debasement, standardized coins, established monopolies in the striking of them, and took steps to prevent wild-cat operations. Banks, as we have seen, began to issue bank notes in the seventeenth century and by then were performing yeoman service in transferring funds by bills of exchange, by "*Giro* banking" (book-keeping cancellations of debts and credits by order of their clients), and by other methods.

Capital was accumulated for investment by banks and then in the seventeenth century by joint stock companies. Here was a business institution, long out of use, which could draw upon the savings of many investors who took shares in an enterprise in the search for profits. Then states, which re-established the public function of taxation as against the feudal practice of taxes for the benefit of the lord, accumulated wealth from their levies and sometimes turned it to investment ends. Finally bourses, or exchanges, came into being in which investors and *entrepreneurs* could meet more readily to borrow or loan or to buy and sell actual goods or shares of stocks or bonds. Attempts were made to minimize risks by the creation of an investment market, the sale of annuities that would assist men in their old age, and by the sharing of risks, particularly as regards sea and fire losses, through the process of insurance.[6]

The development of modern capitalism had a decided effect upon methods of production. In agriculture there was a tendency towards specialization of production to meet urban food demands and to provide industry with some of its raw materials, like wool. Furthermore, relationships between the actual owners of land and peasants became less personal and more and more regulated by money payments. In brief, the entire feudal system, which had been so drastically altered in the fourteenth century, slowly disintegrated under the impact of a money economy. In the nineteenth century, its last vestiges disappeared, and agriculture was carried on according to the tenets of capitalism.

Changes in industrial production were more dramatic than in agricultural production, and they were to have much more far-reaching consequences. Indeed the comparative advantages that

Western Europe was ultimately able to achieve in industry account in large part for the supreme economic position that it attained in the world in the nineteenth century and for the relatively great economic surpluses which it created.

Although the history of European industrial development is a long one and its beginnings reach back to the Middle Ages and in technology even to ancient times, it is especially marked by rapid changes which began to take place in the sixteenth and seventeenth centuries. The demands of overseas areas for European industrial goods exerted pressure upon producers to turn out increasing quantities of such things as ships, ships' stores, hardware, and clothing. Simultaneously the growth of political states and intense rivalry among them increased demands for military supplies, while civilian demand went up, as it usually does when prices are rising. To meet the new demands, there was greater investment in industry, a more extensive division of labour, and an increasing tendency for consumers to obtain what they wanted in exchange for money in an impersonal market.

For the most part the existing guild system was not able to rise to the new challenge, for it was too rigidly bound to the idea of maintaining a monopoly over a small market. A different kind of enterprise system was needed, one that would put greater emphasis on volume of output and less on quality and price restrictions. Private business for profit grew rapidly, facilitated as it was by the existence of more money, instruments of credit, and banking services. *Entrepreneurs* found, moreover, that the guild system had effected a considerable division of labour which could easily be developed further and that guilds had trained labour which they could not absorb and which was ready to be hired for wages. Western Europe was, furthermore, richly endowed with natural resources necessary for industrial expansion. It had iron ore, charcoal and later coal for smelting the ore, timber and resin for ships, and wool for textiles. Finally, Europe had been developing the field of mechanics and had machines, like the hand loom, that could be put to use to produce more goods with less labour per unit of output.

Perhaps it was not until the nineteenth century that Western Europe experienced substantial effects of the mechanization of industry—of what has been called the "industrial revolution"— and not until then did industrial output exceed in value agricultural production. Yet as early as the sixteenth century, if not before, the signs of industrial production organized on capitalist lines were unmistakable. One of the early indications of the trend was the growth of a system by which a business venturer bought materials, placed them in the hands of workers who processed them for him at a price, and then disposed of them in distant markets. Certain guild masters, instead of themselves making goods for local sale, engaged in such practices, but usually non-guild members, especially merchants, were the pioneers. In some instances, the labourers worked up the goods in their homes on their own machines, whence came the terms "domestic system" or "putting-out" system for this form of enterprise, but they might lease machines from their employers or they might congregate in a building owned by the merchant and operate their employers' machines, whence the more appropriate term of "merchant-employer system."

This type of industrial organization was frequent in the textile industries, particularly in knitted goods. In this latter field a mechanical contrivance was developed in the late sixteenth century which was a harbinger of things to come. An Englishman, named Henry Lee, invented a machine that was capable of 1,500 stitches a minute as compared to 100 stitches by a hand knitter. Here was a device that could easily be operated at home and that could enormously increase output. It was just the type of thing that an *entrepreneur* could provide for home-workers in order that they might more cheaply turn his raw materials into finished products.

In ship-building, coal-mining, beer-making, salt-refining, and

certain other industries, where relatively large investment and
continuous operation were required, production was concentrated in one place and was financed by the more wealthy, or by
partners, or later by stock companies. In these industries, technological advances began to appear, such as the use of coal for
heat, pumps for removing water from mines, hoists for lifting
heavy loads, and tracks to reduce the friction of wheels. The
steam engine itself evolved from a machine to pump water from
mines, and the first steam engines used for traction were employed
at the heads of coal mines.

The growth of mechanized, capitalist industry was so important in England from 1540 to 1640 that some scholars speak of an
"early industrial revolution" there between these years. In the
seventeenth century, France made several advances in mechanized
industry, as did the Netherlands and southern Germany. Then
in the eighteenth century, the invention of the spinning jenny,
the flying shuttle, and the power loom revolutionized the textile
trade. The discovery of a method to smelt iron ore with coke
and of machines for working iron more readily entirely changed
the role of metallurgy in Europe's economy. The invention of
the steam engine made possible the production of cheap and
mobile power—power that was available for all kinds of manufacturing processes at almost any location. At last Europe had
developed a means of using on a large scale inorganic materials
—the stored-up resources of nature—for its economic needs.

In the first three centuries of modern times when these
developments were taking place, the modern political state was
coming into being. This new form of political organization was,
of course, much concerned with its economic potential and its
military power. Accordingly the youthful states of Europe
adopted economic policies which they believed would operate to
their best interests. What the specific policies were varied according to circumstances, but they comprised attempts by each state
to retain for itself all or the lion's share of commerce with its

colonies or spheres of influence, to prevent colonies from producing goods which the mother-land could supply, and to encourage production in the colonies of goods, particularly raw products and bullion, for which there was a large demand in Europe. In addition, some states, notably Spain, tried to hoard bullion within their boundaries in the belief that such a policy would redound to their benefit. Some stressed the development of domestic commerce by breaking down internal customs barriers and by improving transportation; others emphasized the necessity of greater agricultural and industrial production; and all sought larger populations in the interest of military might.

These measures have been lumped together indiscriminately under the term "mercantilism," yet no one state pursued each or all concepts with equal vigour. Portugal and Spain stressed bullionism; the Netherlands, free trade and commerce; and Britain and France, the actual production of goods and services. Britain, particularly, placed emphasis upon the desirability of exchanging with other regions its manufactured goods for raw materials and foodstuffs. This concept of productivity as the basis of national wealth stood the test of time, for indeed Western Europe attained its position of economic eminence by becoming the "workshop of the world." In one sense this position of economic supremacy of Western Europe was an aim of mercantilism, for the aggregate of mercantilist policies envisaged the economic development of Europe at the expense of the rest of the world.

From what has preceded, the conclusion can be drawn that economic well-being in Western Europe in the period between 1500 and 1800 stemmed from the exploitation of overseas areas, increased commercial activity, greater industrial production, the extension of the institutions of a money economy, and the greater organization of economic life according to the tenets of modern capitalism. Thus the degree to which successful development along these lines was realized in various parts of Western Europe is a key to determining which places enjoyed the greatest supply of goods and services. In regions of greatest economic development fortunes could most easily be amassed which could be devoted to advances in civilisation.

Civilisation in Western Europe to 1800

The period from the fifth to the tenth century A.D. has been usually regarded as the "dark age" of Western Europe. In these years this area produced relatively little of an indigenous character in the fields of art, architecture, literature, philosophy, or science. In the early part of this period the chief centre of civilisation was at Constantinople, where Byzantine culture preserved much of ancient Greek and Roman learning and added important contributions of its own. Byzantine influence made itself felt in Italy, particularly at Ravenna and Venice, with which Byzantium had political and commercial ties. Yet such influence was so limited that it led to no great period of creative activity in the whole of Western Europe.

Nor did Arabic civilisation, which developed in the sixth century and spread rapidly in the seventh, provide the leaven necessary to start a new cultural movement in Western Europe, although certain of its currents had by the eighth century made their mark in Spain, southern France, and Italy. Troubadour literature of Languedoc, for example, reflects borrowings from Arabian literature; much of Greek philosophy, including parts of Aristotle's, was made known to the West through Latin translations from the Arabic; and Arabic scientists taught Western Europeans some of the natural science which passed current for centuries. The West learned of Galen and Hippocrates from Arabic sources and held Arabic medicine in high esteem. Similarly Western Europe acquired from Arabic civilisation knowledge in the fields of chemistry, physics, astronomy, geography, and mathematics, including "Arabic" numerals.

The first really creative period indigenous to Western Europe began in earnest in the eleventh century and reached its height in the twelfth and thirteenth centuries, when commerce was expanding and towns were growing. Up to that time architecture had followed Roman models in the Romanesque style, but now it acquired originality with the Gothic form. Sculptors and painters began to throw off the rigidities and formalism of Byzantine art and to attain form, expression, and movement. Those trends were apparent in Gothic sculpture, particularly in scenes of the Last Judgment, which so frequently surmounted the main entrances of churches, and in paintings by masters like Cimabue (1240–1301) and Giotto (1266–1336).

French creative activity found literary expression in the love lyrics of the troubadours, which reached their peak in the twelfth century, and in the *chansons*, like the *Chanson de Roland*[7] in France, the tales of King Arthur and his Round Table, *Tristan and Isolde* in France and Germany, and *Reynard the Fox* in the Low Countries.[8] For the most part these works were written in the language of the common people rather than in Latin, and they treated subjects closer to the experience of Western Europeans than had the more classical works of earlier times—facts that contributed to their vitality and success. Upon their heels followed a literary movement in Italy that owed much to the liberal patronage and general encouragement of the Holy Roman Emperor, Frederick II (1211–1250). To his Sicilian court he invited many of the leading writers of his time and there gave impetus to a movement whose most remarkable product was Dante Alighieri (1265–1321). Dante's *Divine Comedy* is an amazing synthesis of the reflection of his part of the Middle Ages and is generally considered to be one of the greatest epics of all time.

The twelfth century also gave a strong impetus to learning. By its end the universities of Bologna, Paris, Montpellier, and Oxford, at least, were well established. To the "schools" came teachers, who had previously given instruction as best they could to groups of followers, to debate theological questions.

Peter Abelard (1079–1142) in his *Sic et Non* presented arguments for and against most of the established beliefs of the Church, and St. Thomas Aquinas (1225–1274) in his *Summa Theologiae* presented logical proofs for the existence of God, the immortality of the soul, and all fundamental propositions of religion. Such intellectual activity, called scholasticism, did not result in an orthodoxy of belief but rather in a heterodoxy—a variety of views and an attitude of questioning. It opened men's minds to the possibility of other than established doctrines, to the world of man, and to physical science.

Interest in the physical world proceeded at first along lines drawn by ancient authors like Aristotle, Galen, and Ptolemy. Soon, however, these "authorities" began to be questioned and corrected as a result of observation and experimentation. Roger Bacon (1214–1294) exemplified the new tendency in his pleas for the use of the "experimental method" and in his personal quest for knowledge. By the beginning of the fourteenth century a correct explanation had been made of the rainbow, revising Aristotle's view; attention was being given to the subject of dynamics through the study of projectiles; and efforts were being expended not only to organize existing knowledge of geography but to extend it by explorations. Furthermore the study of alchemy resulted in the accumulation of information about inanimate nature; the practice of medicine, to closer observation of anatomy and disease; and the development of pharmacy, to an alphabetical listing and explanation of the believed efficacy of drugs.

Following the flowering of cultural activity in the twelfth and thirteenth centuries, sometimes referred to as the Twelfth-century Renaissance, some retrogression seems to have set in. Architectural design, literary form and artistic styles seem to have been worn thin by repetition, and creativeness appears to have lost much of its earlier vigour. Yet the recession was not of long duration, nor was it general in all regions. In Italy, the then

wealthiest part of Europe, a new cultural movement got under
way in the late fourteenth century which was to dominate and
give form to Western European artistic and intellectual life for
the next three centuries. The movement was called humanism,
and the period of its flowering has been called the *Renaissance*.[9]

Humanism sang the praise of Greek and Roman culture,
lauded belles-lettres, and stressed the importance of amenities
in literary discourse. To a degree it was a reaction against the
emphasis that in the twelfth and thirteenth centuries had
been placed upon theology, metaphysics, medicine, and physical
science. Humanists wanted to capture the purity of classical
Latin, and in doing so made Latin a dead language and consequently helped to establish vernaculars as literary languages.
They strove to find, edit, and give currency to Greek and Latin
texts, thus reviving much of the learning of these civilisations.
And they scoffed at the culture of the entire period from the fall
of Rome to their day for the lack of the very things that they
admired, an attitude that laid the basis for the mistaken view
that all the Medieval Period was a "dark age."

Gradually the influence of the humanists began to make itself
felt in Italy and subsequently in the lands to the north and west.
In architecture the graceful Gothic gave way before a revival of
Roman forms with their horizontal lines and massiveness—to
the creation of the Renaissance style. Sculpture lost the imagi-
native quality found in Gothic statues and became more lifelike
or more naturalistic. Painting began to achieve the reproduction
of what the eye actually saw rather than what the artist conjured
up in his mind about what he saw and could only imperfectly
represent because of crude techniques. Literature dealt to a
greater extent with passions and frailties of the flesh and less
with ethereal ideals and other-worldly virtues.

In order to have a vivid image of the changes that were taking
place one has only to compare the massive architecture of St.
Peter's in Rome with the ethereal Gothic cathedral at Chartres,

the stylized sculptures of that same cathedral with the realistic work of Michelangelo (1475–1564), a stiff Byzantine mosaic with the almost photographic quality of a Raphael (1483–1520), the saintly *Summa Theologiae* of St. Thomas Aquinas or essentially religious *Divine Comedy* of Dante with the love sonnets of Petrarch (1304–1374), or the earthy tales of Boccaccio (1313–1375) and Chaucer (1340–1400) with the humanistic works of Erasmus (1466–1536).

Inasmuch as Renaissance humanism stressed values that were at odds with established religion, it contributed directly to the Protestant revolt from the Church. And its praise of Roman history and political concepts influenced the statecraft of rising national political states. Yet its emphasis on the arts and belles-lettres detracted from scientific investigation. This detraction was, however, never complete. Questioning of accepted views went on and with it efforts to find new answers. Doubts about traditional views of geography were instrumental in encouraging explorations; and explorations resulted in startling discoveries. The *Notebooks* of Leonardo da Vinci (1452–1519) bear ample witness to the scientific interests of this extraordinary person and of the society around him. His work in mechanics, botany, zoology, and anatomy indicates a desire for knowledge of the physical world and for acquiring that knowledge by observation, experimentation, and the ordering of data in meaningful relationships. Nevertheless, science of the Renaissance was only a preliminary to the great flowering of this branch of intellectual activity in succeeding centuries.

Undoubtedly the finest achievements of the Renaissance were precisely in those fields that humanists held in highest esteem and which they cultivated most assiduously—in arts and letters. These achievements constituted for most of Western Europe real "golden ages." Italy had such masters in painting as Masaccio (1401–1428), Leonardo da Vinci, Raphael, Michelangelo, and Titian, as well as a host of others. In sculpture she had Donatello

(1386–1466), Michelangelo, and Benvenuto Cellini (1500–1571). In architecture she produced such structures as the dome of the cathedral in Florence, St. Peter's in Rome, and the great colonnade around the court in front of it—the work of Bernini (1598–1680). In literature she had Ariosto (1474–1533) and Tasso (1544–1595). In music, she was honoured by Palestrina (1524–1594) and the originators of the modern opera. And in political science, she could claim Machiavelli (1469–1527), author of *The Prince*.

During the last half of the sixteenth and the first half of the seventeenth century, Spain had its "golden age" with such masters of the pen as Cervantes, Lope de Vega, and Calderôn. In painting it could boast such leaders as El Greco and Velasquez. The Netherlands, both north and south, had their golden age over a longer period, with the Van Eyck brothers and Memling in the fifteenth century, Brueghel and Erasmus in the sixteenth century, and Rubens, Van Dyck, Rembrandt, and Vondel in the seventeenth century. England attained a literary height during the reign of Elizabeth (1558–1603) with Shakespeare, Francis Bacon, Spenser, Marlowe, and Ben Jonson. Portugal produced its greatest literary work, the *Lusiads* by Camoëns, in the sixteenth century, and in the same period Germany had such great painters as Cranach, Dürer, and Holbein, and a number of classical scholars. France had its Rabelais, Montaigne, and Ronsard in the sixteenth century and its great dramatists, Corneille, Racine, and Molière in the seventeenth.

In this very partial list of great figures of the Renaissance appear the names of a large proportion of the most illustrious painters and writers of Western culture. Undoubtedly there was a spirit of the times which inspired these men and a competitive attitude which spurred them to action. Yet it is at least a curious coincidence that several Western European countries achieved such cultural heights at a time of rapid economic development and that the great vitality waned as economic conditions worsened. The last of the great Renaissance figures appeared in Italy in the late sixteenth century; Spain's economic decline was accompanied by a falling off in literary and artistic accomplishment; and the same can be said of Portugal, Germany, and the Netherlands. In England and France intellectual activity continued, although it took a new turn, and these were the very places where economic decline was the least. Finally, sight should not be lost of the fact that those areas of most intense intellectual life after the overseas discoveries were on the Atlantic seaboard.

In spite of the remarkable achievements of the Renaissance, considerable agreement among students of Western culture can be found for the proposition that the most distinctive and, relative to other cultures, the greatest accomplishment of the West has not been in the field of arts or letters but rather in the realm of the physical sciences. In no other culture has there ever been such an extensive sequential ordering of information about the real world, and in no other has there been a comparable understanding of, and control over, things physical.

Because one of the most distinctive and remarkable achievements of Western civilisation has been the development of physical science, its history becomes as much a part of our concern as painting, sculpture, literature, or philosophy. At first glance profound differences might be thought to exist between the natures of aesthetic and scientific accomplishments. On closer observation, however, apparent distinctions appear to be minor. While established styles of art may hamper fresh expression and lead to sterile copying, so also may traditional beliefs restrict scientific investigation. In both fields, advances are dependent upon a large body of data and skills developed through time. Finally, progress in both realms depend in part upon a social attitude which demands vigorous and fresh treatment and upon economic conditions which permit or stimulate cultural activity.

In general, advances in the physical sciences in the sixteenth, seventeenth, and eighteenth centuries occurred in those parts of

Europe where economic expansion was taking place and where ideas were freely exchanged. It was centred at first chiefly in Italy, in the Low Countries, and in scattered commercial centres but later tended to find most congenial conditions in England and France. To the career of Leonardo da Vinci, we should now add that of Galileo (1564–1642), who advanced the study of motion and of astronomy; that of Torricelli (1608–1647), who determined the weight of atmosphere and contributed to the development of the barometer; that of Vesalius of Brussels (1514–1564), who pushed forward the study of anatomy; and that of Mercator (1512–1594), the Flemish geographer, who developed a system for projecting the earth's form upon a flat surface.

To be sure, there was Copernicus (1473–1543), a native of Cracow, who advanced the theory that the sun is the centre of the solar system and that planets revolve around the sun; but Cracow can be classed as a commercial centre, and furthermore, Copernicus got much of his training in Nuremberg and in Italy. Then there were in the early period Tycho Brahe (1546–1601), a Danish astronomer, and Kepler (1571–1630), his assistant, who through observation and calculation proved Copernicus to be correct and who described mathematically the orbits of the planets.

Subsequently there were Descartes (1596–1650) of France, who preached the virtues of the scientific method; Harvey (1578–1657) of England, who discovered the circulation of blood; Robert Boyle (1627–1691), who raised chemistry from pharmacy and alchemy to the level of a natural science; and Sir Isaac Newton (1642–1727), who set forth the general theory of gravitation and who devised calculus, the mathematics necessary to describe motion. Leeuwenhoek (1632–1723) of the Netherlands was the first to discover bacteria and the first to describe human spermatozoa; Priestley (1733–1804) experimented with gases and discovered oxygen; Cavendish (1731–1810) isolated hydrogen;

and the Frenchman Lavosier (1743–1794) may be said to have developed quantitative analysis. Linnaeus (1707–1778) of Sweden systematized botany; a score of workers established the science of geology; and Benoit de Maillet (1656–1738) suggested that existing species of living things had been produced by changes in preceding species, thus anticipating the theory of evolution.

These and many other discoveries not only extended man's knowledge of the physical world, but they also laid the foundation for a still vaster expansion of natural science in the nineteenth and twentieth centuries. Such knowledge had two important consequences: first, it permitted man greatly to increase his control over nature; and second, it led to new concepts regarding religion, the universe, and human behaviour. Scientists seemed able to establish that the physical universe operated according to laws which could be described mathematically and which appeared to be eternal, immutable, and natural. In fact, Newton went so far in describing the world as a machine that he effected one of the most influential intellectual transformations of all time—the Newtonian revolution.

If natural, eternal, and immutable laws regulated the physical world, it was possible that the same was true of the world of man, or at least so many persons came to think. Accordingly a search for these laws characterized much of the activity of philosophers at the end of the seventeenth and in the eighteenth centuries. Among the pioneers was John Locke (1632–1704), who attempted to explain the laws by which stimuli, or sensations from material things, combined to form the mind, memory, thought, and character of the adult. Similarly, he endeavoured by the use of reason to discover "laws" regulating the formation of social institutions and political organizations. In the same vein Diderot (1713–1784), the editor of the *Encyclopédie*, and his fellow workers on this great compendium of eighteenth-century knowledge sought to describe human behaviour.

As corollaries to these efforts to portray the universe as a mechanical contraption, God's existence was doubted or flatly denied. Voltaire (1694–1778) argued brilliantly that God should be regarded merely as a first cause—a "watch-maker" who had set the mechanism going and then had left the machine to run by itself according to eternal, immutable, and natural laws. Then so much faith came to be placed in nature that with Jean Jacques Rousseau (1712–1778) we encounter an advocate of a return to it and a condemner of the artificialities of man-made institutions. Thus much was done to question irrationally held beliefs and to prepare the way for wider acceptance of knowledge arrived at by empirical means.

Unquestionably the outstanding artistic accomplishments of the eighteenth century were not to be found in architecture, sculpture, painting, or belles-lettres,[10] for each of these branches was bowed down by traditionalism. Few would deny that the most distinctive literature came from the pens of rationalists, who were primarily concerned with social science, history, or philosophy, and that the most illustrious artistic achievements were in the field of music. Probably it is correct to state that the chief centres of musical output were in Germany and Austria, where economic development had reached a point at which it could support the arts. Handel (1685–1759), although he was attracted to England, was born in Prussia and received part of his training in Hanover; Bach (1685–1750) was a Saxon; Beethoven (1770–1827), a native of Bonn; and Mozart (1756–1791) and Haydn (1732–1809), Austrians. The works of these men are generally recognized as being at the summit of all musical literature.

The great accomplishments in the arts and sciences from the Dark Ages to 1800 might never have been realized had there not been a remarkable extension of "control over human environment," that is, an expansion of the range of opportunities for developing the creative talents of individuals. With the breakdown of feudalism from the Black Death onward, individuals began to acquire more freedom of action, and human conduct came to be regulated by more generally recognized laws. Many of the religious curbs on thought were diminished by scholastic disputations, by the Protestant revolt from the Church in the sixteenth century, and by philosophies urging the use of the scientific method. Physical scourges were reduced by better sanitation and medicine; and even warfare probably was not worse than it had been earlier in spite of new tensions among the growing national states and the appearance of the forerunner of "total warfare" during the French Revolution.

Finally, progress towards political equality and towards the participation of all in public affairs was remarkable. In some places, for example, in Venice and Genoa, oligarchical republics were established; and in others, like France, national monarchies replaced feudal rule. In most countries the new national kings attempted arbitrary government, but their efforts met stiff opposition. The belief developed that the individual had certain "natural, eternal, and immutable rights," like life, liberty, the pursuit of happiness, and the possession of property, and that no authority could infringe upon these gifts of nature. If one did violate them, then revolt against established authority was permissible. Furthermore these doctrines were accompanied by demands for the extension of political privileges to a larger proportion of the population and for the formation of public policies by the duly elected representatives of this broadened electoral base. With the Glorious Revolution in England in 1688, with the American Revolution of 1776, and with the French Revolution of 1789, these demands were in part realized, and the principles upon which they were based were more firmly established. Thus the nineteenth century was ushered in by a political system which increased the individual's responsibilities and gave him an opportunity to improve his condition and his society.

From this survey of Western culture in the period between the fall of Rome and 1800, certain facts emerge which require especial emphasis. Economic progress appears to have been given an initial impetus by commerce between distant places. Commerce, in turn, increased when one area possessed or could obtain goods that were known to be in great demand in another area and when transportation of these goods was possible both politically and economically. Consequently, technological advances in transportation and in the production of goods, as well as political arrangements permitting commercial intercourse, were crucial matters. Furthermore, one of the striking aspects of this history was the effect that a relatively small volume of trade had in changing economic institutions. This phenomenon is to be explained primarily by the fact that trade greatly extended the range of economic opportunities and brought into being a class of businessmen—the merchants—whose task it was to make the most of business opportunities. For a long time merchants were pioneers in accumulating and investing capital in both trade and industry with the avowed purpose of reaping a profit.

With the growth of trade and of industry, towns increased in size, and in the urban areas there took place a division of economic and intellectual labour. Here we find again the chief centres for the achievement of those things that we consider to be marks of civilisation. We also have found a considerable correspondence in time and place between general economic well-being and the creation of masterpieces in the arts and sciences. Again we introduce our frequently repeated caveat that economic surplus to support intellectual and artistic activity could be amassed by a few at the expense of the many and that the problem of such accumulation depended upon political and social conditions as well as upon economic factors. Finally, we have encountered once more the question of why and how a society develops goals, patterns of thought, and styles of expression. Our analysis is not aimed to deal with these questions in detail, but we have indicated shifts from the Dark Ages to a Christian-Gothic-scholastic culture, then to the humanistic-classical-Renaissance pattern, and finally to the mechanistic-scientific. From the last point, we move to a consideration of the history of Western culture in the last 150 years.

1 Some trade over long distances was always maintained, especially trade in salt, pepper, incense for church services, and grain in times of famine.

2 At this time there were no locks. Dams were constructed at intervals to maintain a water level on canals. These dams were passed by means of an inclined plane and winches to pull up or let down the barges.

3 They, in turn, probably obtained it from the Far East.

4 Contrary to views that were held for a long time, the fact that Turks conquered Constantinople in 1453 seems to have had little to do with the case. Turks had been active along many of the Near Eastern trade routes to India for a long time and did not relish the thought of destroying a trade that was profitable to them.

5 A bank note, like any other credit instrument, is in essence a promise by someone to pay a stipulated sum. A bank may issue paper notes to a greater amount than the gold and silver in its coffers, even if it promises to redeem the bank note in bullion, because *all* holders of its bank notes would not usually demand the bank to meet all its promises to pay at one time. Probably the first true bank notes were issued by the Bank of Stockholm in 1661.

6 For a bona fide insurance contract, five elements must be present: (1) the insured possesses an interest of some kind that can be estimated in money terms; (2) the insured is subject to risk of loss or impairment of this interest; (3) the insurer assumes risk of loss; (4) such assumption is part of an arrangement to distribute actual losses among a large group bearing similar risks; (5) as consideration for the insurer's promise, the insured makes a ratable contribution, called a premium, to a general insurance fund from which claims of loss are paid.

7 It was written prior to the close of the eleventh century.

8 *Reynard the Fox* was probably not written until the thirteenth century.

9 The use of the word "renaissance" for this period has been severely criticized because it implies the absence of a revival in the twelfth and thirteenth centuries. The term has become too well established to be abruptly discarded, but clearly the *Renaissance* was a new *Renaissance*.

10 Even the works of Reynolds, Romney, and Gainsborough in England can hardly be considered an exception, although they gave England what is sometimes called the golden age of English painting.

For Further Reading

J. N. L. Baker, *History of Geographical Discovery and Exploration* (1937)

Shepard B. Clough and Charles W. Cole, *Economic History of Europe* (1946)

A. Dopsch, *The Economic and Social Foundations of European Civilisation* (1937)

E. J. Hamilton, *American Treasure and the Price Revolution in Spain, 1501–1650* (1934)

C. H. Haskins, *Medieval Culture* (1929)

C. J. H. Hayes, *Historical Evolution of Modern Nationalism* (1931)

J. Huizinga, *The Waning of the Middle Ages* (1924)

Archibald Lewis, *Naval Power and Trade in the Mediterranean, A.D. 500–1100* (1951)

Eli Lipson, *Economic History of England* (1929), 2 Vols.

John U. Nef, *War and Human Progress* (1950)

Henri Pirenne, *Economic and Social History of Medieval Europe* (1937)
——— *Medieval Cities: Their Origins and the Revival of Trade* (1925)

J. H. Randall, *The Making of the Modern Mind* (1940)

Henri Sée, *Modern Capitalism* (1928)

Percy Sykes, *History of Exploration* (1935)

John A. Symonds, *Short History of the Renaissance* (1894)

H. O. Taylor, *The Classical Heritage of the Middle Ages* (1911)

The Cambridge Economic History of Europe (1942 *ff.*)

The Cambridge Medieval History (1913–1936), 8 Vols.

James Westfall Thompson, *An Economic and Social History of the Middle Ages* (1928)

Lynn Thorndike, *History of Magic and Experimental Science* (1923–1941), 6 Vols.
——— *A Short History of Civilisation* (1948)

A. A. Tilley, *Studies in the French Renaissance* (1922)

A. A. Wolf, *A History of Science, Technology, and Philosophy in the Sixteenth and Seventeenth Centuries* (1935)

VII

WESTERN CULTURE IN THE NINETEENTH AND TWENTIETH CENTURIES

THE historian of the mid-twentieth century who studies the economic development of Western culture of the last 150 years is struck at once by the enormous quantitative increase in the production of goods and services. Just how great the increase was is difficult to state in precise terms, but for Western Europe it has been perhaps in the order of six to eight times. At least what evidence we have indicates more than a doubling of French national income from 1850 to World War II, a quadrupling of that of Germany for the same period,[1] a tripling of that of Italy from 1860 to 1938,[2] and an eightfold increase in that of the United States from 1869–1878 to 1929–1938.[3] Such increases made possible a rise in the population of Europe from some 187,693,000 people in 1800 to over 530,000,000 in 1938 and in the United States from 4,000,000 in 1790 to 140,000,000 in 1946. Over the entire period there was an increase in income per capita of population of some two to four times.

The last 150 years

This expansion in physical production, in population, and in goods and services per capita does not have a parallel in all history. Such being the case, the curious man of the second half of the twentieth century can properly demand that the historian explain how this unique phenomenon came to pass.

The main lines of explanation are not difficult to perceive. First, much of the increase in production resulted from the mechanization of industry. By means of the machine, driven by mechanical power, the individual operator could produce a quantity of goods that by any other system would have required tens, hundreds, or even thousands of workers. The single workman came to have a multitude of mechanical slaves to do his bidding.

Second, the increase in goods was made possible by using on a scale never dreamed of before the stored-up riches of nature— the mineral resources of the earth. Hitherto most of man's economic wants had been supplied by plants or animals, supplies that were limited by available man-power, arable land, rainfall, and the growing qualities of strains and breeds. In the last century and a half, however, man has been able to dip into the "capital" of nature and thereby to have a new and additional, although not inexhaustible, supply of materials for his use.

Third, improved methods of transportation and communication made possible the tapping of resources over a larger portion of the earth's surface. Products from far-distant places, whether timber from high mountain ranges or from jungles, grains from remote corners of the earth, or coal deep underground were made accessible to men. And as though this were not enough, new knowledge about the growing of crops and the raising of animals permitted a phenomenal increase in the production of agricultural products on land that had been tilled for centuries.

In brief, then, the great increase in goods and services between 1800 and 1950 may be attributed primarily to the mechanization of industry, the greater use of inorganic matter, improved agricultural technology and the tapping of resources over a greater portion of the globe. In this generalization, however, three aspects of economic development in the 150 years in question are not adequately recognized. The first of these is that the new economy required a greater division of labour or specialization of tasks than had ever before been realized; the second is that the division of labour and the bringing into the market of greater supplies of goods from a larger portion of the earth was made possible by improved means of transportation and a vast extension of trade; and the third is that trade could not imaginably have been conducted without money and elaborate banking services.

Great as was the increase in goods available for human use in Western culture after 1750, all parts of that culture did not experience economic expansion at the same time or in the same proportions. The movement was most marked at first in England, then in Belgium and France, and subsequently in Germany, Italy, the United States, and other nations. It was so located, however, that Western Europe achieved a predominant world position of economic and political-military power. In 1821 Great Britain and France alone took 92 per cent. of American cotton exports, which was about one-half of the United States' total crop. In 1870, the United Kingdom, Germany, France, Belgium, Italy and Sweden had 61 per cent. of the world's manufacturing production and the United States 23·3 per cent. of it. In 1840 the United Kingdom alone had 32 per cent. of world trade, France 10 per cent. and the United States 8 per cent. Furthermore, the states of Western culture acquired such economic-military power that they were able to exert their authority outside that culture almost at will. In fact, they extended their domination over a large portion of the globe in a second great wave of imperialism between 1870 and 1914.

As time went on, however, Western Europe failed to maintain its *relative* economic position in Western culture, or, for that matter, in the world. The United States moved rapidly to the fore, with most of the world aping or trying to ape Western culture's productive technology. By 1913 the United Kingdom, Germany, France, Belgium, Italy, and Sweden accounted for 41·9 per cent. of world manufacturing production, the United

States for 35·8 per cent. and Russia for 5·5 per cent. In 1936–1938 these percentages were 29·7, 32·2, and 18·5, and for Japan 3·5 per cent.[4] Whereas the percentage of world trade accounted for by the United Kingdom, Germany, and France was 43 per cent. in 1890, these same countries did only 36 per cent. of that trade in 1913, and 26·9 per cent. of it in 1938. The entire trend towards the development of industry outside Western Europe is exemplified by these statistics.

Other elements in the European picture also looked black—and one of the blackest was nationalism. Within Europe a system of political states had developed in which each nation claimed its sovereign right to act in its own interests irrespective of the welfare of others. For the most part, the people of Europe had an emotional, if not a fanatical, feeling towards their nation-states. Nationalism made difficult and, indeed, almost precluded inter-state co-operation : and it was a serious contributor to war. In this regard an interesting parallel can be drawn between Europe and ancient Greece. Like Greece, Western Europe has failed to achieve political unification ; and internecine strife has weakened it to a point where invasion by another culture is a real threat. Such has become the economic, political, and military plight of Western Europe that it is almost certain to see the leadership in Western culture pass to the English-speaking people of the northern part of the Western Hemisphere. Up to the eve of World War II, however, the peoples of Western culture were much better off materially than were those in any other culture, and especially well off were the populations of the United States, Canada, New Zealand, the United Kingdom, and Switzerland.

The question now remains whether or not this economic well-being per capita has been accompanied by remarkable achievements in the arts and sciences. As to the latter, there can be no question. Never before has man been able so fully to order events sequentially, to explain their inter-relationships, or to control his physical-material environment. As to accomplishments in the arts, there is great difference of opinion. Standards of aesthetic judgment are so highly subjective that a scientific appraisal of the art of the last 150 years is nigh impossible. Nor in this case, because it is so recent, can we turn to historical literature to discover whether or not works of art in the period have been universally and consistently considered great in comparison with the creations of other cultures. We shall have to await a future historian with the advantage of more hindsight than we possess to have recourse to this method. Yet we may hazard a guess regarding his findings. It may well be his judgment that relative to earlier periods within Western culture, artistic accomplishments in the West during the last 150 years have considerable merit. Impressionism in painting, the symphony and opera in music, and functional building in architecture will probably stand the test of time.

Our future historian's severest strictures of recent Western culture will probably relate to politics and philosophy. So far Western nations have failed to settle their differences peaceably, and unless they overcome this weakness they may destroy themselves in combat or they may become so weak that peoples of another culture will prey upon them. Nor at present does Western culture have a philosophical system to which its members all adhere and for whose ends its people strive. Material betterment seems to be the predominant goal of life, but such a goal leads to differences and conflicts among both social and political groups and even between Western cultures and other cultures. How man is to get along with man, and group with group, are the major unsolved problems of our day. Indeed, they have been major problems throughout all history.

Mechanization of industry

As has already been said, the last 150 years have witnessed the most rapid and extensive technological changes to be found in an equal period of time in all man's recorded past. This statement can be made without fear of contradiction in spite of the fact that, because technological innovations are dependent upon earlier achievements, no two changes are strictly comparable. The scope and effects of automatic textile machines, of the steam engine, of cheap methods of making steel, of the electrical dynamo, of the internal-combustion engine, and of nuclear fission have been enormous. In the author's opinion they surpass accomplishments in the thousand years prior to 3000 B.C.—a millennium that saw the development of copper and bronze metallurgy, the harnessing of animal power, the making of brick, and the use of the wheel in pottery and transport.

The explanation of the more recent changes in technology is of necessity extremely complex, for a myriad of factors and forces combined in the right proportions and with a favourable timing to produce the new ways of making things. The major factors involved can be classified as follows : (1) capital or surplus that could be used to develop, construct, and put into operation new techniques ; (2) the capitalist spirit or the desire for gain and material benefit from the use of new methods of production ; (3) technical knowledge which made possible improvements in performing certain tasks ; (4) markets or a demand for goods greater than could be met by older forms of production ; (5) workers who were willing and able to operate the new machines ; (6) a sufficient and steady supply of raw materials.

By the eighteenth century these factors were present to a considerable degree in various parts of Western Europe but particularly in England. There capital had been amassed through trade, handicraft production, seignorial payments, tax collecting, and banking, and methods had been developed for putting capital to work. The capitalist spirit had grown apace as land as a source of wealth, social prestige, and political power had given way to trade and industry. Technical knowledge had increased through experience with handicraft contrivances and through speculation and experimentation regarding the physical world. Markets had grown with the expansion of Europe overseas, with the development at home of better transportation, and with a tendency of individuals to specialize in the production of one or a few things and to satisfy their other needs by purchases. Workers were available at money wages from handicraft industry, from agriculture, and from the not fully employed child and female segments of population. Finally, a sufficient supply of raw materials was made possible by increasing production of them and by commerce.

Conditions seem, indeed, to have been ripe for technological change, and change did take place. This was the beginning of the "industrial revolution"—a revolution which did not occur so suddenly as is frequently thought and which even yet has not run its full course. Although no one factor acted as the sole catalytic agent to effect the mechanization of industry, the invention of machines and processes of production were so crucial to the "revolution" that they deserve our special attention.

What we call inventions come about from the accretion of many details, which, when finally put together, result in something new. They do not pop suddenly and fully developed from the head of some isolated genius but are related to some problem or process for which a solution is being sought. In turn, the actual adoption of inventions depends upon the need for them, their effectiveness in meeting this need at lower costs, the ability of workers to use them, and the willingness of those with capital to put them into operation.[5]

In the eighteenth and early nineteenth centuries those persons who were accumulating details about machines and industrial processes were mostly handicraftsmen rather than highly trained engineers and scientists. Inventions came in those crafts where rudimentary machines were already in use, where productive methods were not rigidly fixed by tradition or law, and where workers could easily adapt themselves to the new contrivances.

14

And they appeared and were put to work in industries where the demand for goods was great in relation to supply, especially in staple industries with mass markets. Thus, among the first machines of the "industrial revolution" were the spinning jenny, the flying shuttle, the power loom, the circular saw, the rotary planer, puddling in iron smelting, screw- and nail-making machines, the coking of coal, the harrow, iron ploughs, and the slide rest for metal-turning lathes.

Successful inventions tend to have a cumulative effect, for changes in one aspect of production create pressures for changes elsewhere. Thus, many of the early machines were designed to be activated by human energy, but they were so constructed that the application to them of energy from inorganic sources was an obvious step. Accordingly power from the existing water wheel was used on them at an early date, but because the location of water wheels was restricted to places with falling water and because the supply of water depended in many cases upon the vagaries of the weather, there was need for a supplementary or substitute source of energy. This need was met by the invention of the Watt steam engine in the 1770's and the subsequent development of that machine.

The steam engine was itself an agent for rapid change. It came to produce power cheaply from an inorganic substance in abundant natural supply ; it was mobile enough to be used where there was sufficient fuel and water ; and it was adaptable to many uses, both as a stationary power unit and as a portable machine that could propel itself. Its adoption made possible the factory system on a large scale, cheaper and faster transportation, and an increase in the production of goods per unit of human input.

The application of more power and the attainment of higher speeds in industry necessitated, in turn, the construction of machines from more durable materials than wood or cast iron. Steel seemed to be the answer to this problem, but steel was too expensive until Bessemer (1856) and Siemens and Martin (1866) developed their respective processes of steel-making. Their inventions led to a 50 per cent. decline in the price of steel from 1856 to 1870.

In another respect, too, the new methods of making steel were an important landmark in industrial history. They illustrate a movement that had been taking shape and that was henceforth to be highly characteristic of technological change, that is, for inventions to be made by trained scientists rather than by handicraft mechanics. Industrial machinery and processes were becoming so complicated and highly specialized that the worker was seldom able to provide solutions to any except the more rudimentary problems that he encountered. In fact, nearly all basic technological changes after the middle of the nineteenth century must be attributed to men of science. They were responsible for the technical development of electricity and the internal-combustion engine. They created countless new machines and increased the efficiency of earlier ones. They effected the "chemical revolution" which permitted the production of useful goods from materials in abundant supply. They were able to effect an "agricultural revolution" that has increased productivity of land and animals beyond the dreams of our forefathers. And they are credited with the "physical revolution," which has extended greatly man's control over nature and which through nuclear fission bids fair to provide mankind with an important new source of energy and of materials. In brief, men of science have facilitated the output of more goods and services per unit of human input through better and fuller use of nature's resources.

The agricultural revolution

Important as was the mechanisation of industry in providing members of Western culture with a surplus that would permit them to devote time and energy to artistic and scientific activity, it was by no means the only source of increased wealth. It was accompanied, indeed, by agricultural changes which have been glorified by the term "revolution." This revolution began, like the industrial revolution, in England, in the eighteenth century. At its origins it consisted primarily in the use of machines drawn by animals, the introduction of new crops, better care of animals, and selective breeding. As it progressed, it was characterized by the application of science to a wide range of agricultural problems and to extensive mechanization of agricultural processes.

Farm machinery was improved and made more useful, especially with the development of the tractor. Many new crops were introduced, such as the sugar beet, and older ones, like the potato, were more widely cultivated. Better grains were grown, and legume crops, like alfalfa, which are less exhaustive of the soil than others, were more generally grown, while hybrid seeds proved highly productive and resistant to drought and blights. Animal and plant diseases and pests were brought under greater control by the use of new medicines, insecticides, and fungicides. Breeding was greatly improved through more rigid controls, artificial insemination, and the discovery that individual stock had different abilities in passing desired qualities to its offspring.

Furthermore, science discovered the chemical requirements of plants, which led to extensive changes in the use of fertilizers, especially commercial fertilizers. New attention was given to land utilization, that is, to those particular types of land that were best suited to different kinds of agriculture, and subsequently to reafforestation, irrigation, and drainage projects. Finally, greater care was exercised in the processing of foodstuffs, such as the pasteurization of milk, the storage of grains, and the making of sugar from beets.

These various changes had dramatic results. The production of grains per hectare just about doubled in Western Europe

during the period under consideration, and the average would
have been greater if so much marginal land had not been kept
under the plough. Less food was necessary for draught animals
after the use of the tractor became generalized. More emphasis
was placed upon animals that produced food, like cattle, poultry,
and pigs, than upon those that were raised in part for an industrial raw material, like sheep. And these changes effected some
alteration in human diets, with a trend towards protective foods,
which are high in vitamin content, and away from foods eaten
mainly for their calorific value.

The agricultural revolution had profound effects upon costs
of production for different types of crops. Through the use of
machines, grain, for example, could be grown most economically
on large tracts by means of extensive agriculture, while poultry
and vegetable farming could be conducted profitably on small
holdings by intensive farming. The importance of these changes
became clear in the 1870's and 1880's, when American grain
came into Europe on a large scale. In some European countries
the reaction to overseas agricultural competition was to protect
traditional crops by tariffs or subsidies ; in others, it was to
concentrate efforts on those products in which intensive agriculture had a comparative advantage. If the former policy were
adopted, prices for basic commodities were higher than on the
world market ; if the latter course were taken, the country in
question had to export its surpluses and import what it did not
produce. High prices meant a disadvantage ; while reliance on
imports meant dependence on foreign suppliers and their willingness to take industrial goods.

In Western Europe farming was mostly on a small scale
and of the intensive variety, for in this way a larger total output
of farm products was possible and greater employment opportunities were provided. Much of the land was in small holdings,
and what was not was usually cultivated in relatively small
units by tenants or share-croppers. Thus European farmers had

difficulty in mechanizing agricultural work, because the size of their enterprise was not great enough to carry machinery. Western Europe lost its early agricultural advantages based on technological advances to other areas of Western culture, but its agricultural production per worker remained high compared with that in non-Western cultures.

Trade and the division of labour

With all its advances in technology Western Europe would not have been able to achieve a position of economic primacy in the world without trade. Only by means of an enormous expansion in the exchange of goods was it possible for Western Europe to get foodstuffs and raw materials for its use in return for manufactured goods. World manufacture is estimated to have increased 740 per cent. from the period 1870–1880 to the years 1936–1938 and intra-national trade to have expanded even more than this, but international trade grew by only 300 per cent.[6]

Important in the growth of commerce were improved methods of transportation, a greater use of money as a medium of exchange, bank credit for financing commerce, and a vast network of distributing services, but the points that require emphasis in the present context are (1) that commerce greatly furthered the division of labour and (2) that it led to multi-lateral trade among the various nations of the world.

How extensive the division of labour became can be judged by a comparison of the percentage distribution of the gainfully employed in a highly industrialized country like Germany with similar percentages in a non-industrialized country like Mexico.

	Year	Agri-culture, Fishing	Mining	Manu-facturing	Commerce & Transport	Adminis-trative, Domestic Service, Etc.
Germany	1933	29	4	36	19	12
Mexico	1930	68	1	13	7	11

The figures for Germany, if broken down still further, would show how very little of the production of the average worker was consumed directly by him and how dependent he was upon the market for his numerous needs. Consequently the individual operative in industrialized regions was better able than workers had ever been before to specialize in some aspect of production and by integrating his efforts with others to increase his productive capacity. Indeed, there has been a high correlation between those countries with an extensive division of labour and those with high incomes per capita.

Similarly multi-lateralism in international trade meant that various parts of the world could specialize in the production of various goods in which they had a comparative advantage and through exchanges get the things that they did not produce. Thus the United States could acquire raw rubber from the Malay Peninsula, the Malay Peninsula could obtain consumer goods from the United Kingdom, and the United Kingdom could receive grain from the United States. Each area got materials that it needed, and if the system worked perfectly, there would be a multi-lateral balancing of debits and credits.

As the workshop of the world Western Europe enjoyed many advantages. One peculiar one was that the terms of trade favoured industrial areas rather than agricultural, or, to put it another way, prices of industrial products were higher than foodstuffs or raw materials when measured in terms of human input. Yet this situation gave non-industrialized countries an incentive to manufacture for their own needs and hence to weaken Western Europe's economic position. Furthermore, Western Europe's primacy was undermined by another factor. In its exchange of manufactured goods for foodstuffs and raw materials, Western Europe did not export goods equal in value to its imports, the difference being made up by various "invisible" items such as emigrant remittances, earnings on insurance, shipping services, tourist expenditures, and earnings on investments. In the final balance of payments Western Europe had for a long time a creditor position and kept investing overseas, a practice that hastened industrialization elsewhere. [7]

The industrialization of the rest of the world had an impact upon Europe's position and upon a pattern of trade that had come into existence. This pattern was also distorted by sudden technological changes or political events, like war. Thus the industrialization of the United States altered Europe's economic role in South America ; the two world wars deprived Western Europe of many of its overseas markets ; and these same con- flicts led Europe to spend so much of its overseas investments that it no longer had large earnings from them to help pay for imports. Finally, depressions, especially that of the 1930's, caused a decline in international trade far greater than in domestic commerce as nation after nation sought in the emergency to protect its national economies.

Tariffs, and later, import quotas and currency controls were employed either to hasten industrialization or to meet the exigencies of sudden dislocations. While trade could usually become adjusted to mild protection, it could not cope with absolute limitations. Beginning with World War I the con- tinuation of the system of multi-lateral trade and payments was threatened ; and in the 1930's and 1940's multi-lateralism was almost destroyed by restrictions of various kinds. Western Europe suffered particularly from this turn of events because of its large dependence on foreign areas as markets and as sources of supply. Only with the existence of multi-lateralism can Western Europe retain some semblance of the economic position that it previously enjoyed.

Desire for material betterment—savings and investment

Another important element in the economic expansion in Western culture during the last 150 years was the desire of people for material betterment. Ever since the appearance of humanism in the Middle Ages, a concept had taken form and assumed importance in Western culture that a perfectly legitimate interest of man was man, that man's full potentialities could not be realized by scorn for physical well-being, that man should seek a full, creative life here and now because of uncertainties regarding the hereafter, and that eternal salvation, if such there be, was not reserved for the poverty-stricken. Certainly by the end of the eighteenth century one of the fundamental ideologies of Western culture was to seek better material conditions on this earth.

In the presence of such an ideology, there were few indeed who did not strive consciously to improve their lot. The capitalist spirit was a vigorous agent of economic growth. It accounts, in part, for those captains of economic activity who specialized in making decisions that would increase their wealth. It accounts, in part, also for the willingness of large numbers to save from their current earnings in order to invest their surplus in the hopes of greater supplies of goods in the future. This process of savings and investments was about as crucial to economic expansion as were inventions, for without it a hand-to-mouth existence is inevitable. What the rate of capital formation was throughout the 150 years under consideration it is impossible to say, but it has been estimated to have been 12 to 15 per cent. of national income in the United States for the years 1869 to 1938.[8]

Whatever the rate of capital formation was, however, it was enormous compared with that of any other culture, either contemporary or past. Savings were possible in large part because the supply of goods increased so much more rapidly than population that people could maintain a standard of living to which they had become accustomed and at the same time put something aside for the future. Furthermore, an increase in real wages and a growing population meant a greater demand for goods, which in turn encouraged the making of new investments. In brief, savings did not cause additional hardships, and a comparatively widely distributed, increased purchasing power stimulated the flow of savings into productive enterprise.

Obviously not all savings went directly into capital goods for the production of still more goods. A considerable amount was devoted to other than economic activity, which allowed achievements to be made that are marks of civilisation. Large sums were devoted to education and research which permitted the talents of a larger proportion of the population to be developed than ever before, which provided scientific training for further control of environment by man, and which stimulated artistic creativeness. Yet the proportion of available earnings used for non-economic purposes did not prevent economic expansion, as they did perhaps in Egypt in the third millennium B.C. when the great pyramids were constructed. Western culture has to a large extent in the last 150 years been able to eat its cake and have it too. It has had savings for capital investment and also for intellectual and artistic accomplishments. To an imposing degree it has combined economic aims with intellectual or artistic activity through functional, that is, economically useful, art and through science.

The greatest waste of savings has come from preparation for and waging of war—especially the two world wars of the twentieth century. Even though the countries involved were able to regain pre-war levels of production within a decade after the conflicts, thus indicating the recuperative powers of Western culture's economies, the retarding effects of war on Western Europe have been tremendous. Furthermore, business fluctuations, which seem to be engendered by the operation of our capitalist system, have troughs during which our human, technological, and natural resources are not fully utilized and during which savings necessary for economic investment or achievements of an artistic or intellectual character are very low. Finally, the concentration of economic power in the hands of a few and the dependence of proletarians on wages for existence have resulted in conflicts of interest that have occasioned waste through strikes, lockouts, and inefficiency. The general historical picture of the last century and a half is a bright one, but it has its sombre parts and some very black spots.

Natural resources and the location of industry

The bringing together at any one place of materials necessary for the production of goods is of great importance to the understanding of the development of industry in Western Europe and the subsequent growth of economic activity in the United States. Although steam shipping, steam railroads, motor trucks, and high-power electric-transmission lines have reduced the cost of transporting goods and energy and have made the location of industry more flexible, proximity to materials that are bulky and heavy in relation to their value or the value of what is made from them is a decided advantage. In fact, even today industrial activity tends to be concentrated relatively near them or in places to which they can be brought cheaply, usually by water.

Of all such raw materials coal was king and iron ore queen. In 1938, four-fifths of inorganic energy used in industrialized European countries came from coal,[9] and almost all machines and tools were made from steel. Any industrial map of Western culture will show how industry has grown up around coal and steel-making regions—in the Ruhr of Germany, in the north and east of France, in the Midlands in England, and in the eastern part of the United States. As it happens, Western culture has a great advantage over other areas in the matter of coal and steel, for over half the known coal resources of the world are located in it, and prior to World War II some two-thirds of world production came from Western Europe, the United States, and Canada. Also these same regions contain more than half the known iron ore reserves of the world and in 1947 produced some 80 per cent. of the world's steel. These advantages contributed to the concentration in Western culture of the lion's share of the world's manufacturing production.

The accompanying table makes clear not only the predominant industrial position of Western culture but also shifts in the relative industrial importance of various regions. Of particular significance to our study are (1) the percentage decline of manufacturing production in Western Europe, especially in the United Kingdom and France ; (2) the percentage increase of manufacturing in the United States ; and (3) the percentage growth of industry in areas outside Western culture like Russia and Japan. These charges are altering the power potentials of states and the economic base of cultural achievement.

Why these shifts took place can be explained in broad terms by the extent to which factors of production came to be present in the more recently industrialized areas. More specifically they can be understood primarily from an investigation of the "process of diffusion" of mechanized industry—from a study of those elements of industrialization that were propelled outward by the earlier industrialized areas and of those forces in the so-called backward areas that led to borrowing from industrialized areas. Basic to such a study is the migration of machines and techniques.

The first mechanized processes to be adopted by non-industrialized areas were those closely connected with handicraft production. Information about the new machines was easily obtained, was readily understood by handicraft workers and engineers, was applied without great capital investment, and pertained to industries for whose goods there was a large native demand. Thus textile machines were in the first group to migrate, along with such things as the circular saw, tools for installing and repairing simple machines, and more rudimentary forms of transportation.

From such beginnings the skills of workers and engineers gradually increased so that they could use more complicated machines and techniques. What was then introduced depended upon the natural resources, transportation facilities, market opportunities, and cultural desires of the area in question. By

PERCENTAGE DISTRIBUTION OF THE WORLD'S MANUFACTURING PRODUCTION*

Period	United States	Germany	United Kingdom	France	Russia	Italy	Canada	Belgium	Sweden	Finland	Japan	India	Other countries	World
1870	23·3	13·2	31·8	10·3	3·7	2·4	1·0	2·9	0·4	..		11·0	12·3	100·00
1881-85	28·9	13·9	26·6	8·6	3·4	2·4	1·3	2·5	0·6	0·1		12·0	12·0	100·00
1896-1900	30·1	16·6	19·5	7·1	5·0	2·7	1·4	2·2	1·1	0·3	0·6	1·1	12·3	100·00
1906-10	35·3	15·9	14·7	6·4	5·0	3·1	2·0	2·0	1·1	0·3	1·0	1·2	12·0	100·00
1913	35·8	15·7	14·0	6·4	5·5	2·7	2·3	2·1	1·0	0·3	1·2	1·1	11·9	100·00
1913†	35·8	14·3	14·1	7·0	4·4‡	2·7	2·3	2·1	1·0	0·3	1·2	1·1	13·7	100·00
1926-29	42·2	11·6	9·4	6·6	4·3‡	3·3	2·4	1·9	1·0	0·4	2·5	1·2	13·2	100·00
1936-38	32·2	10·7	9·2	4·5	18·4‡	2·7	2·0	1·3	1·3	0·5	3·5	1·4	12·2	100·00

League of Nations, *Industrialization and World Trade*, 1945, p. 13.

*Includes finished products, semi-manufactures, like unworked metals, pulp, coke, fertilizers, and cement, as well as manufactured foodstuffs, like flour, canned goods, and sugar.

†The second line for 1913 represents distribution according to frontiers established after World War I.

‡U.S.S.R.

the middle of the twentieth century it was no exaggeration to say that technological knowledge could be quickly and widely diffused. No one area could long maintain an industrial advantage based solely on knowledge.

Why the earlier industrialized countries permitted this diffusion of industrialization is not difficult to discern. They were willing to sell machinery and knowledge to other areas to maximize profits, to get materials that they wanted, or to lift backward areas to their level of civilisation. For similar reasons, these same industrialized countries were willing to invest capital in backward countries, thus providing these regions with a start that would have been greatly delayed if reliance had been placed solely on native capital formation.

With the diffusion of Western technology there has arisen in backward regions a realization that industrial production is necessary for rapid economic growth and for the conduct of modern warfare. And most important of all, perhaps, there has spread throughout the world a cultural belief in the desirability for material improvement. The world is becoming mechanized and to a degree Westernized—and in this process Western culture has lent a helping hand. Whatever the virtues of such a policy may have been, that policy has tended to weaken the relative economic position of Western Europe and to shift the economic centre of gravity in Western culture to the northern part of the Western Hemisphere.

Population and labour

Thus far in our discussion of the economic development of Western culture we have considered the role played by technological advances, by capital accumulation and investment, by the desire for material betterment, by the division of labour made possible through specialized production and trade, and by raw materials. We have also endeavoured to show how

Western Europe achieved first a position of world economic primacy by means of a fortunate combination of the factors of production and also how this position was weakened as other areas became industrialized. We come now to a consideration of the relationship of population to economic growth and to civilization.

As an historical proposition one may say that given equal technology, an equal desire for material improvement, and fixed natural resources, a population that is relatively sparse will increase its productivity per capita more rapidly and to a greater degree than a population that is relatively dense. In the former case, trade and a division of labour develop early which permit capital accumulation, while in the latter case a large portion of the population remains in self-sufficient agricultural pursuits, trade is slight, and capital accumulation difficult and slow. If it is a truism that a population that approaches the limit of its resources, including its technology, tends to be more static economically than a population far from such limits, it is a truism that deserves reiteration.

At the beginning of the nineteenth century Western Europe's population was not close to the limits of its resources, for technology and trade were making new resources available. This situation was conducive to economic growth and economic growth to increases in population. From 1850 to 1900 the rate of population increase was 1 per cent. per annum, but by the beginning of the twentieth century the *rate of increase* began to decline, particularly in Western Europe, and by the 1930's the populations of some Western European states were nearly stable. Western Europe was approaching the limits of its economic resources, and many people, especially members of the middle and upper middle classes, wanted to protect their own standards of living by having fewer children.

In the United States and Canada limits of economic resources to population were much farther away than in Europe, and in these countries population increases were especially dramatic and have not reached their climax. The population of these countries rose from about 5,000,000 in 1800 to 160,000,000 in 1949, and the rate of increase is about 1·4 per cent. per annum, compared with about 0·5 per cent. in all of Europe. These countries benefited from a large immigration, the United States having received 38,000,000 Europeans from 1830 to 1930. In an economic sense, Europe was thus exporting a valuable, for emigrants were mostly of productive ages and the country of origin bore the cost of rearing that was not made up by emigrant remittances. Such movements of population undeniably assisted the United States and Canada in their economic growth *vis-a-vis* Western Europe. Incidentally immigrants brought with them heterogeneous skills and ideas, and heterogeneity is believed to have been a stimulating factor economically and culturally in the New World.

If the United States and Canada had an advantage over Western Europe in that their populations were relatively sparse compared to their economic resources and in that they received immigrants of productive ages, they profited perhaps less from the fact that the mean ages of their populations were lower. From Roman times to 1800 life expectancy at birth did not vary much from twenty-five years. Just before World War II, however, life expectancy at birth in Western Europe was about 62·2 years and in the United States 63·8 years. Undoubtedly a higher mean age of the population has meant greater productivity per capita, for older persons have greater skills and make fewer mistakes than younger ones and a smaller proportion of the population is in unproductive early ages. In time the mean age of a population may become so high that speed and strength are markedly diminished or that a large proportion of the population will be unproductive because of old age. This danger has only recently seemed very real. Of greater concern has been a fear that, whereas an increased mean age may permit a larger use by artists and scientists of their skills, it may lead to less innovation of new styles and ideas and to stereotypes.

Whatever the effect of longer life of populations may be culturally or economically, it is still a fact that those things that Western culture considers to be marks of civilization are products of urban societies. Even with improvements in transportation and communication and with many rural areas having urban tastes and patterns of life, this generalization holds true. Thus it is significant that with the various population changes already discussed, there was a steady trend towards urbanization. In 1800 only about 20 per cent. of the population of Western Europe lived in towns of more than 2,500, while in 1948 some 60 per cent. lived in such communities. In 1790 only 5 per cent. of the population of the United States lived in towns of 2,500 or more, while in 1940, 57 per cent. lived in agglomerations of this size or greater and 29 per cent. lived in cities of 1,000,000 or more.

Thus general population changes tended to favour economic development, particularly in the United States and Canada, and to enlarge the environment in which cultural activity flourishes. At the same time the labouring elements of the population were undergoing changes that made them more productive. Not only was labour distributed occupationally so that it could use its energies more effectively, but it was given an opportunity to master economic arts to an ever-increasing degree. Western culture embarked during the nineteenth century upon a programme of mass education that had never been equalled. More people were taught to read and write, illiteracy dropping from more than 60 per cent. of the population at the beginning of the nineteenth century to less than 6 per cent. of the population at the mid-point of the twentieth century. Literacy permitted workers to extend their knowledge of economic activity—to learn about their trades from the printed page.

In formal educational institutions attention was given to vocational training so that workers could acquire the fundamentals of their crafts quickly, and at a low cost to society. Apprentice training, in-training, "growing-up" in a trade, and similar practices meant the development of skills within a larger portion of the population. The simplification of tasks performed by a larger percentage of labour through the mass production of goods on assembly lines required less specialized training for the rank and file but higher skills for the few.

Accompanying these changes, there was also, for a long time, at least, an increasing willingness or necessity on the part of labour to turn out goods and services. As ownership of the means of production shifted from workers to capitalists, workers became largely dependent for existence upon their wages. If they did not work steadily, they did not eat, while formerly they had been able to loaf for considerable periods if they had amassed enough surplus for their needs. In short, the wage system drove men to work. Furthermore entrance to most trades was free, and the worker who wanted to better his lot had the possibility of advancement to more remunerative callings.

Even after the development of highly organized labour unions with their hostility to "speed-ups," with their protection of certain trades and positions for their members, with such uneconomic practices as "feather bedding," and with such economically wasteful weapons as the strike, the above generalizations remained essentially true. The power of labour and its unproductive policies will have to become much stronger than they are before a radical decline in productivity can be attributed to them.

Nor under the system which has prevailed has labour failed to better its lot. The number of hours worked per annum has fallen from 4,000 in 1800 to 2,000 in 1937, and the real wage

MIDDLE EAST

EUROPE

AFRICA

GREENLAND

Atlantic Ocean

SOUTH AMERICA

CANADA

UNITED STATES

ALASKA

Pacific Ocean

SIBERIA

PHILIPPINES

CHINA

AUSTRALIA

NEW ZEALAND

proletaria

PRESENT EXTENT
OF WESTERN CULTURE

of labour has about doubled since the beginning of the nineteenth century.

The most important impediments to production, so far as labour is concerned, are to be found in its social attitudes, such as hostility to the capitalist system and to capitalist employers, opposition to the introduction of new methods of production, reluctance to leave a depressed economic area for a more active one, and awareness of the lack of adequate incentives for greater output. In general, however, the most important hindrances to the productivity of labour are to be found in the absence of opportunities to work accompanying depressed periods of economic activity. Indeed one of the major problems in Western culture has been so to order economic life that the fullest use of economic resources may be possible and commensurate with the desires of its population for goods.

Concentration of wealth

Remarkable as was the expansion of economic production in Western culture from 1800 to 1950, first in Western Europe and subsequently in the United States, Canada, Australia, and New Zealand, it was not so astonishing as the remarkable increase in production per capita with its augmentation in goods available for individual use. Contrary to what had so frequently been the case in previous cultures, populations did not grow so rapidly that economic gains were absorbed by new consumers. But wealth was not so evenly distributed that increases per capita resulted only in a marked improvement in the standard of living for all. In fact, wealth was concentrated enough so that surplus could be used for providing leisure to a comparatively large number of persons for the pursuit of artistic and intellectual activity.

Just how concentrated wealth was can be illustrated in the cases of Great Britain and Paris, France.

GREAT BRITAIN, 1924-1930 (PERSONS OVER 25 YEARS OF AGE)

Capital Group	Percentage of Total Number of Persons	Percentage of Total Capital for Group
£100 or less	76·3–78·6	3·6–6·1
£101–£1,000	15·5–17·3	10·4–11·1
£1,001–£5,000	4·2–4·6	17·0–17·7
£5,001–£10,000	0·8–0·9	10·0–10·3
£10,001–£25,000	0·5–0·6	14·4–14·8
£25,001–£100,000	0·2–0·3	18·6–19·1
Over £100,000	0·04–0·05	23·2–23·8

DISTRIBUTION OF PERSONAL WEALTH AMONG SOCIAL CLASSES IN PARIS, 1930, 1931

Size of Fortune (francs)	Number of Persons	Amount of Wealth (francs)	Per Cent of Total Number of Persons	Per Cent of Total Amount of Wealth
0–50,000	2,663,431	8,136,958,826	94·1	7·65
50,001–500,000	128,929	21,306,896,762	4·7	20·02
500,001 and over	32,416	76,968,910,305	1·18	72·31

Clearly, concentrated wealth permitted its owners to purchase the works of artists and intellectuals, to subsidize their activities through educational institutions, and to provide leisure to family members for work that was not immediately economically rewarding. Furthermore, the state through the great extension of its scope of action provided its members with many cultural opportunities—through its educational structure, its theatres and musical activities, its buildings, and its adornment of public property. In America, public-school buildings have been referred to as the "cathedrals" of the modern age, and a similar statement could be made regarding public building generally in Western culture. What is more, tax-supported cultural undertakings aimed to develop talent wherever it could be found, irrespective of the social and economic status of persons involved. Probably never in history had a parallel attempt been made to discover and train the best-qualified persons in society and to provide them with opportunities for creative activity.

Finally, business has probably supported the arts and sciences to a larger degree than in any of the other cultures that we have studied. Inasmuch as economic enterprise has been organized on such a vast scale, it has built great office structures, imposing factories, and enormous railway stations, stores, and warehouses. To the erection of these buildings some of Western culture's leading architects and masters of the plastic arts have lent their talents. So, too, in the design of products and in advertising, gifted persons have found opportunities for expressing themselves or for making a living that allowed them to engage in creative work of their own.

Between business and physical science, relationships have been even closer. As has already been indicated, most of the great inventions and discoveries of the past hundred years have been the work of scientists. Men of affairs wait breathlessly for the findings of scientists doing basic research to extend man's knowledge of the world around him ; and scientists have collaborated with businessmen in efforts to find solutions to practical operational problems. It is not an exaggeration to say that recent science and art in Western culture are highly functional, that is that they are useful and are integrated with economic activity.

Achievement in the arts

Economic surplus that permits leisure for artistic and intellectual pursuits is not a guarantor of great achievements. It is fundamentally a permissive factor, albeit an essential one. The quality of artistic and scientific production depends on a myriad of other factors, such as the abilities of the artist or scientist, opportunities for the exchange of ideas, and the presence of a competitive spirit that drives artists and scientists to improve their work. Much depends also on the standards of workmanship and the patterns of style that are inherited from the past, borrowed from other cultures, or newly generated. The effectiveness of actual accomplishments will also hinge upon the degree to which creative work is in harmony with the basic ideologies of a culture and upon the extent to which it appeals to such fundamental psychological drives as hunger, sex, and fear, or to human experience in society relevant to these forces. The quality of scientific activity depends, on the other hand, upon the degree to which scientists make possible an extension of human control over physical and social environment for the welfare of all.

In any attempt to evaluate aesthetic and intellectual achievements of Western culture in the last 150 years, one has inevitably to face the knotty problem of determining the boundaries of that culture. Although the chief areas of the Western world are easily recognized, there are borderline districts, like Russia, where Western influence has been very great and where many of the leading artists and scientists have behaved much like Westerners but in which the general pattern of culture is not Western. Similarly individual workers in cultures even more different than Russia from the West may have received training in Western culture and, as borrowers, may have created great works in the Western tradition. Whatever may be the merits of including such persons in any general survey of artistic and scientific accomplishment, we have excluded them here as not being relevant to our basic concern.

Artists in Western culture of whom we shall treat were all subjected to classical art forms as passed on by humanists of the late medieval and early modern period and as transformed during the seventeenth and eighteenth centuries. Yet many of them in the period now under consideration broke away from slavish attachments to classical traditions. As persons in a dynamic and changing environment they altered the old styles and generated drastically new ones. In literature, for example, men of letters liberated themselves from classical rigidities and developed a new form of expression—the novel—in which they found boundless freedom. Novels might be short or long, descriptive or narrative, and limited or unlimited in time and place. They might deal with any subject—history, everyday life of people, social problems, or the inner workings and emotions of the human mind. Brilliant use of this literary device was made by men like Victor Hugo (1802–1885), Giosué Carducci (1835–1907), Gustave Flaubert (1821–1880), Thomas Hardy (1840–1928), and Thomas Mann (born 1875).

Trends, similar to those discernible in the novel, were also to be found in poetry and drama. Among many distinguished masters, we may mention Johann Wolfgang Goethe (1749–1832), a great and sensitive poet, who in *Faust* could analyse the ruminations of the mind over a universal problem, and George Bernard Shaw (1856–1950), a genius in the dramatization of social and political issues and in the satirical questioning of many of Western man's irrationally accepted concepts.

In music, as in literature, there were breaks with tradition and a search for new forms obtained by volume, discordance, and rhythm. In opera there were Richard Wagner (1813–1883) and Guiseppe Verdi (1813–1901) ; in symphonic and chamber music, Johannes Brahms (1833–1897), Frédéric Chopin (1810–1849), Hector Berlioz (1803–1869), and Claude Debussy (1862–1918) ; and in jazz, George Gershwin (1898–1937).

In the plastic arts a great transformation took place. By the early nineteenth century, pioneer painters were seeking to convey an impression of what they saw (impressionism) rather than a mere photographic likeness, and successors endeavoured to express what they felt or thought about what they saw (expressionism, futurism, and surrealism). New strength and originality were thus added to art by such men in painting as Eugéne Delacroix (1798–1863), Édouard Manet (1832–1883), Claude Monet (1840–1926), Pierre A. Renoir (1841–1919), Henri Matisse (born 1869), and Pablo Picasso (born 1881); and in sculpture by Auguste Rodin (1840–1917) and Aristide Maillol (1861–1944).

Architecture suffered from ornate and gaudy buildings constructed along Renaissance lines, like the Opera House in Paris (1861–1875), from stereotypes of the Gothic style, like the Riverside Church in New York, or from copies of classical and neo-classical buildings, like government offices in Washington, D.C. Yet architecture was able partially to free itself from earlier models and by becoming highly functional developed styles of grace or of imposing mass. Urban dwelling units in the Netherlands planned by Berlage (1856–1934), the skyscrapers of Rockefeller Centre in New York built in the 1930's, the work of Auguste Perret, the public buildings of Charles Le Corbusier (born 1887), and factories, like the Industrial Tape Corporation's plant at New Brunswick, New Jersey, are all cases in point.

How well these structures, or for that matter, how well literature, paintings, sculpture, and music, will stand the test of time we cannot say. Judgment at present is warped by a great conglomeration of inferior work which all too frequently blinds us to the good. Mass education has led to a plethora of art for consumption by those who can read and write but who are untutored in regard to fine, artistic craftsmanship or who lack appreciation for other than the simple and obvious. It may be that this fact has led to a deterioration of literature through the popular novel, of the theatre through the moving picture, of music through jazz, of painting through advertising art, and of architecture through hasty construction to meet rapidly expanding needs. The fact remains, however, that art for the masses has not prevented great accomplishment, nor is this art entirely void of appeal to basic psychological forces.

Control over physical and human environment

Whatever the final verdict may be regarding art in the years since 1800, one may be certain that future judgments concerning the extension of human control over physical environment will be extremely favourable. Much of this extension was of an economic character and has already been dealt with in our discussion of economic progress, but part of it was non-economic and of a more purely scientific nature.

As we have already seen, the nineteenth century inherited a desire to learn more about the physical world and a tradition of collecting observed data, of arranging those data in sequence, and of investigating meaningful relationships among them. This tradition was strengthened by the high place given to science in the dominant philosophies of the time, from the positivism of Auguste Comte (1798–1857) to the pragmatism of William James (1842–1910) and the instrumentalism of John Dewey (born 1859). Even those who criticized complete reliance on rationalism, like Immanuel Kant (1724–1804), Friedrich Hegel (1770–1831), and Henri Bergson (1859–1941), recognized the fabulous accomplishments which could be achieved in its name.

One cannot contemplate the names of the great scientists of the last 150 years without being amazed at the contributions made to the extension of man's control over his physical environment. One stands in awe before such men as Michael Faraday (1791–1867), who got mechanical motion from electrical current ; Justus von Liebig (1803–1873), who developed soil chemistry and discovered the basic chemical ingredients of plant food ; Thomas Edison (1847–1931), who invented the incandescent electric light ; Louis Pasteur (1822–1895), who worked out the chemistry of fermentation ; Charles Darwin (1809–1882), whose theory regarding the origin of the species stimulated work in genetics ; Pierre Curie (1859–1906) and his wife Marie (1867–1934), who discovered radium ; Albert Einstein (born 1879), who developed the theory of relativity ; and many more too numerous to mention here.

Some notion of the progress made in science can be gleaned from the fact that, while Aristotle was able to enumerate about 500 species of animals and Linnaeus in 1758 could list 4,236 species, Pratt in 1911 was able to name 522,400. Nor should we forget that naturalists have succeeded in making plants and animals produce more things useful to man, astronomers in measuring with a high degree of accuracy stars millions of miles from the earth, physicians in freeing man from many maladies, chemists in deriving useful substances from hitherto useless materials, and physicists in splitting the atom and thus in forming new material. Nor should we fail to recognize the enormous achievements of engineers in transporting electricity over long distances, in bridging rivers, in mining nature's capital, in irrigating deserts, and in building a great variety of machines. So great have been advances in science and in the application of scientific knowledge that modern man controls nature more completely than any of his predecessors.

Understanding of human behaviour that is essential for an increase of man's control over human environment has also been remarkably extended since 1800. Psychologists have been able to describe the physiology of human action and of learning, to understand more thoroughly the processes of action, and with Sigmund Freud (1856–1939) to penetrate even into the unconscious mind. Economists from Adam Smith (1723–1790) to John Maynard Keynes (1883–1946), and not excluding Karl Marx (1818–1883), have sought comprehension of the operation of the ever-changing economic system. Political scientists from at least John Stuart Mill (1806–1873) have acquired a more complete understanding of politics. Sociologists have greatly extended our knowledge of how men live together in society. And historians have vastly augmented our information of how people have behaved in the past.

Fortunately Western culture has adopted several principles of conduct that have been conducive to the attainment of higher levels of civilization. For example, life, liberty, and the pursuit of happiness have come to be regarded in Western culture as rights that cannot be taken away without due process of law. Participation of the individual in the political affairs of the state has been enormously expanded, and this movement has increased the individual's sense of civic responsibility, and has led to the adoption of public policies for the development of the individual's talents and for the improvement of his welfare. The state has taken on not only the task of educating its members but also of looking out for their physical, mental, and moral well-being. Indeed the concept of the welfare state has to a marked degree become generally established throughout large parts of Western culture.

Against these positive factors in human organization must be set some very important negative ones. Tensions have developed among groups that consider themselves rivals for material betterment, as, for example, between labour unions and employers or between the "have-not" and the "have" nations. Changes in living habits, particularly those that provide anonymity and freedom from family discipline, have resulted in anti-social conduct. In some extremely congested urban areas and in periods of great social upheavals, crime and other manifestations of social disorganization are tremendous. Then, too, among negative factors in human organization must be included extreme forms of nationalism—a blind, irrational, and emotional attachment to one's nationality and a belief that the advancement of that nationality's place in the world is the goal of human endeavour. To this kind of chauvinism must be attributed a large portion of the blame for international friction and for the disastrous world wars of the first half of the twentieth century.

Unfortunately social science has been less successful in coping with these problems than physical science has been in dealing with physical questions. To be sure, the social scientist has learned much about the behaviour of individual humans and of human groups, has adopted the scientific principle of arranging data sequentially, and has shown relationships among these data. Accordingly he has become able to explain how a society is constructed, how its ideologies, institutions, and leaders influence behaviour ; how its economic apparatus functions ;

how its political life is managed ; and what the links are among all these aspects of social existence. Indeed the social sciences have become more empirical and less speculative than they once were—and more analytical and less exhortatory. Yet social scientists, unlike natural scientists, are unable except in a limited sense to control their subject matter, which is human-kind. For the most part public policies are fashioned by leaders rather than by social scientists, and the influence of the latter upon the former is usually indirect.

When all is said and done the nineteenth and twentieth centuries will probably not be considered in the future to have been so bleak as many contemporaries have thought and they may, indeed, seem very great compared with the seventeenth and eighteenth centuries. In any case the centre of artistic and intellectual activity will be found to have been in Western Europe where, during the major part of the period, most of the wealth was and the strongest traditions for creative activity were.

In retrospect and in prospect

In the preceding pages we have seen pass in rapid review a large part of the recorded economic past of those cultures which had the greatest influence on Western culture.[10] Our fundamental purpose has been to investigate what correspondence, if any, there has been between periods of economic well-being when there was leisure for other things than just eking out a living and the attainment of the highest stages of civilization. The pursuit of this purpose involved us at once in a statement regarding the meaning of civilisation. We found that in Western culture, at least, degrees of civilisation are measured by the extent of control over physical and human environment and by the quality and quantity of intellectual and aesthetic accomplishments. Our task also involved us in a study of factors of economic growth, of factors of economic decline, and of those specific economic conditions that influence directly stages of civilisation.

We have now reached a point where general statements regarding our findings are in order. As a rule, the historian is more reluctant than other social scientists to make general statements concerning human behaviour, for he knows what a small portion of human experience is available to him and how crucial may be a bit of missing data. Furthermore he recognizes that no situation is ever exactly duplicated in time, for people change and relations among techniques, resources, ideologies, and leaders are so complex that the chances of exact repetition are infinitesimal. Yet in spite of the fact that history never repeats itself exactly, enough similarities occur in analogous situations to permit generalization. Finally, it seems appropriate that general statements based on historical data be formulated by historians rather than by other social scientists who are less familiar than they with the records of the past.

In both economic development and in the attainment of relatively high degrees of civilisation, advance depends to a large extent upon the range of opportunities for alternative decisions. In intellectual and aesthetic accomplishments the extent of this range is determined by the amount of economic surplus which permits of freedom from working exclusively to obtain the necessities of life. Economic surplus should be sufficient or so concentrated as to allow the training of a group of scientists and artists numerous enough to stimulate one another to creative activity. Furthermore economic surplus should be adequate to permit the educating of a large part of society so that it can appreciate or make use of the intellectual and aesthetic creations of scientists and artists. One reason why so many intellectual and artistic achievements have been realized in cities is because these conditions have been most fully met in them.

The range of opportunities for alternative decisions depends also upon the degree of freedom of thought and action that exists in society. There is considerable evidence to indicate that freedom fluctuates along with economic surplus, but economic well-being is in this case not necessarily the chief determining factor. In the formative period of any culture, patterns of behaviour become more or less firmly established, and if these patterns restrict opportunities for alternative decisions, they invariably detract from the attainment of a high state of civilisation. If, on the other hand, patterns of behaviour favour individual freedom, encourage civilising creativeness rather than, for example, the satisfying of animal appetites, and if they promote the use of the best techniques and the adoption of the highest artistic standards of the past, they add immeasurably to the extent to which human energies are devoted to the building of a higher civilisation.

The idea of individual freedom as a factor in civilisation is related to our concept of "control over human environment" as a mark of civilisation. By this is meant the organization of society in such a way that differences among individuals and groups may be at a minimum and that what conflicts do exist may be settled in an equitable manner according to previously established rules. Finally, we mean by "control over human environment" a situation in which society is so organized that the civilising talents of all are developed to their fullest extent and in which policies that might prevent further advance are not pursued.

Our concept of "control over physical environment," although it is meant to be broad enough to include the prevention of disease and the forecasting of the weather, is closely related to economic progress—to increasing the supply of goods and services available per capita in society. Economic progress we found to be dependent on a variety of factors in a variety of combinations. In two periods, in the millennium prior to 3000 B.C. and in the four and a half centuries since 1500, the development of new techniques was crucial in economic progress. In other periods existing techniques were adopted by people who had not had them previously, or they were used more intensively and extensively by those who already possessed them. We found also that savings and investment were important in economic progress, especially investments in commerce and in capital goods. We ascertained, too, that economic progress was greatly advanced by a division of labour that permitted individual workers to specialize in those tasks for which they had the greatest facility. The division of labour had trade as a concomitant, and trade permitted drawing upon the natural resources of a large area and the specialization of different areas in the production of those things for which they had a comparative advantage. Commerce was, in turn, facilitated by means of transportation, communication, money, and banking services for transferring credit.

In general, economic decline can be accounted for by the reverse of those factors of economic progress that we have just mentioned. Retrogression may, however, come about by a rapid increase in population without a corresponding increase in the supply of goods, or by devastating war, or by social disorder. It may result from savings being diverted from investment in capital goods to expenditures on art and knowledge, which we consider to be marks of civilisation. In fact, this process helps to explain the long-term fluctuating character of civilisation. Finally, economic decline may follow the diffusion of one culture's techniques to another culture. In this case, the second culture may be able by means of its acquisitions and other resources to surpass the first culture and possibly to prey upon it.

Our study seems to show clearly that economic well-being is one of the necessary conditions for a high stage of civilisation. At least, we have found a remarkable correspondence between periods of high productivity of goods and services in a culture and its periods of greatest achievement in controlling human environment and in creating intellectual and aesthetic works of a high order. No matter how important the economic factor is, however, other forces are obviously involved. A culture inherits part of its art forms, social goals, and ideologies from preceding cultures ; it borrows part of them ; and it creates part of them.

No matter how it gets them, it behoves man to select his standards well and to foster those forces that lead to greater accomplishment, if he would raise civilisation to a higher plane.

Now that the end of our study has been reached, one may legitimately ask whether or not our findings can be used to answer those questions regarding the position and future of civilisation in Western culture that most perplex modern man. Can they be employed to evaluate the place of Western culture in the present world ? Can they throw light upon shifts in leadership within Western culture ? And can they serve as a gauge that will indicate probable developments in the near future ?

If we answer these questions in the affirmative and then apply our principles to the present situation, what do we find ? First, we may decide that by our definition of civilisation Western culture has now the highest civilisation of any culture in the world. It has the greatest control over both physical and human environment and is accomplishing more in the arts and sciences than any other culture. It has the highest incomes per capita and in view of rapid population increases elsewhere will probably continue to have them. So outstanding are its economic accomplishments and its civilising achievements that its technology, many of its institutions, and some of its ideologies and art forms are being adopted by peoples in other cultures. In fact, the diffusion of Western culture throughout the world is one of the important phenomena of our time.

Second, it is apparent that major changes are taking place in the location of the greatest amount of economic well-being and military power within Western culture. Western Europe has clearly lost the position of overwhelming economic superiority that it enjoyed a hundred years ago. Other areas have forged ahead economically because of their superior resources, superior organization, or greater desire for material betterment. In the meantime Western Europe has not been able to draw upon the natural resources of the entire world in the proportions that it had earlier, partly because of war, partly because of the growing industrialization of backward areas, and partly because of its inability to pay for imports. Economic leadership has definitely shifted to the English-speaking people of North America. Consequently our findings suggest that the centre of civilisation in Western culture will be transferred to the United States and Canada, but this change will take place at best gradually and then only if ideologies and styles leading to high civilisation become firmly established in the New World. If earlier patterns are repeated, however, Western Europe should still have a period of great civilising accomplishment. Only if that area is further wracked and ruined by war is it probable that such a development will not take place.

Lastly, it is possible that as peoples outside Western culture acquire and perhaps improve upon Western culture's methods of producing goods and of waging war, these peoples will become embroiled with the West in war. At least in all the cases that we have passed in review in these pages, cultures with inferior civilisation but with growing economic power have always attacked the most civilised cultures during the latter's economic decline. The chance that this may happen again is so great that enormous amounts of human resources will undoubtedly be dissipated during the coming years in preparation for war. Indeed, the threat of war, as well as actual war, is the greatest present impediment to advances in civilisation both in Western culture and in all the leading cultures of the world.

FOOTNOTES TO CHAPTER VII

1 Colin Clark, *Conditions of Economic Progress*, Macmillan & Co. Ltd., London, 1940, pp. 107 and 95.

2 F. Coppola D'Anna, *Popolazione, Reddito, e Finanze Publiche dal 1860 al Oggi*, Partenia, Rome, 1946, pp. 57–58.

3 Simon Kuznets, *National Income*, National Bureau of Economic Research, Inc., New York, 1946, p. 32.

4 From League of Nations, *Industrialization and World Trade* (1945), p. 13.

5 S. C. Gilfillan, *The Sociology of Invention*, Follett Publishing Co., Chicago, 1935.

6 *Industrialization and Foreign Trade*, League of Nations, New York, 1945, p. 14.

7 For example, Great Britain's foreign investments in 1913 were said to have been £3,763,000,000, or nearly 25 per cent. of national wealth.

8 Simon Kuznets, *op. cit.*, p. 53.

9 In the United States in 1945 only about 50 per cent. of energy used came from coal. Forty-five per cent. came from petroleum and natural gas, and 5 per cent. from water power. *Historical Statistics of the United States, 1789–1815*, Government Printing Office, Washington, 1949, p. 155.

10 We have omitted from our consideration the culture of China, India, Byzantium, and Arabia and of the Mayans and Incas because data regarding their economic development are few and because the inclusion of them would have extended this book beyond desirable limits.

FOR FURTHER READING

G. A. Baitsell, *Science in Progress* (1945)

Charles A. Beard, *Idea of National Interest* (1934)

J. H. Clapham, *An Economic History of Modern Britain* (1938), 3 Vols.

T. Craven, *Modern Art* (1934)

Merle E. Curti, *The Growth of American Thought* (1943)

B. F. Fletcher, *A History of Architecture on the Comparative Method* (1948)

Helen Gardner, *Art Through the Ages* (1948)

S. Giedion, *Mechanization Takes Command* (1948)

Industrialization and World Trade (League of Nations, 1945)

Simon Kuznets, *National Income* (1946)

P. H. Lang, *Music in Western Civilisation* (1941)

Paul Mantoux, *The Industrial Revolution in the Eighteenth Century* (1927)

National Income Statistics of Various Countries (United Nations, 1949)

Karl Nef, *An Outline History of Music* (1935)

The Network of World Trade (League of Nations, 1942)

V. L. Parrington, *Main Currents in American Thought* (1930), 3 Vols.

W. A. Robson, *Civilisation and the Growth of Law* (1935)

Bertrand Russell, *A History of Western Philosophy and Its Connections with Political and Social Circumstances from the Earliest Times to the Present Day* (1945)

Henri Sée, *Histoire économique de la France* (1942), 2 Vols.

The Economic History of the United States (1945 *ff.*)

A. Sartorius von Walterhausen, *Deutsche Wirtschaftsgeschichte, 1815–1914* (1923)

Chester W. Wright, *Economic History of the United States* (1941)

Erich W. Zimmerman, *World Resources and Industries* (1951)

INDEX

DATE DUE